# Coastal Lives
## A Memoir

# Marjorie Simmins

Pottersfield Press, Lawrencetown Beach, Nova Scotia, Canada

Library and Archives Canada Cataloguing in Publication

Simmins, Marjorie, author
    Coastal lives : a memoir / Marjorie Simmins.
Includes bibliographical references.
ISBN 978-1-897426-54-8 (pbk.)

1. Simmins, Marjorie.  2. Cameron, Silver Donald, 1937-. 3. Journalists--Canada--Biography.  4. Nova Scotia--Biography.
I. Title.
PN4913.S495A3 2014                070.92              C2013-907925-4

Cover design by Denise Saulnier and Gail LeBlanc

Cover image: Karen Justice http://www.flickr.com/photos/just-look-photog/sets/

We acknowledge the financial support of the Government of Canada through the Canada Book Fund for our publishing activities. We acknowledge the support of the Canada Council for the Arts, which last year invested $157 million to bring the arts to Canadians throughout the country. Nous remercions le Conseil des arts du Canada de son soutien. L'an dernier, le Conseil a investi 157 millions de dollars pour mettre de l'art dans la vie des Canadiennes et des Canadiens de tout le pays. Pottersfield Press recognizes the support of the Province of Nova Scotia through Film and Creative Industries Nova Scotia. We are pleased to work in partnership with the agency to develop and promote our creative industries for the benefit of all Nova Scotians.

Pottersfield Press
83 Leslie Road
East Lawrencetown, Nova Scotia, Canada, B2Z 1P8
Website: www.PottersfieldPress.com
To order, phone 1-800-NIMBUS9 (1-800-646-2879) www.nimbus.ns.ca

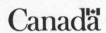

The Canada Council   Le Conseil des Arts
for the Arts         du Canada

Canadä

FILM & CREATIVE INDUSTRIES
NOVA SCOTIA

*For Don, who fell from the sky – love you big as the sea.*

# CONTENTS

The essays in *Coastal Lives* were previously published in *Saturday Night, The Vancouver Sun, Canadian Living, The Horscope, The Chronicle Herald, National Post,* and the anthology *Untying the Apron: Daughters Remember Mothers of the 1950s* (edited by Lorri Neilsen Glenn, Guernica Editions, 2013).

# PROLOGUE

I imagine him sometimes, on that day his hand hovered over the telephone. *So nervous*, he said, months later, *my heart jumping all over*. Was he rocking in that squeaky office chair of his? He would have been smoking, definitely. Maybe he glanced out his ocean-facing window, looked for a Cape Islander boat, a bright bit of moving colour to carry away his anxious thoughts. I see him turning away from the window one last time, squaring his shoulders to the desk. He stretches out his hand and again, pulls it back. Then a deep breath and his fingers are on the keypad. He presses in a number he has already memorized. In several hard heartbeats his phone call travels four thousand miles from the village of D'Escousse, Cape Breton Island, and rings another phone in a suburb of Vancouver, British Columbia. It was 11:00 p.m. AST, 7:00 p.m. PST time. Or maybe a few minutes past the hour. The supper-time news had just finished.

"Hello?" I said – and instantly changed my life forever.

"Hello," he said – and did the same.

Marjorie Simmins and Silver Donald Cameron, on a spring day in the Annapolis Valley, 2012. (Photo by Geoffrey Simmins.)

# 1

## WINTER DAYS IN HALIFAX

*JANUARY 7, 2011, HALIFAX, NOVA SCOTIA*

The rhododendron bush in the front yard is getting whiter by the moment. Its narrow oval leaves are drooping from the cold and are snow-sprinkled as though with fluffy sea salt. There are two yew bushes that flank our front door; the one on the left, which I can see from my workroom window, is even whiter than the rhododendron leaves. The fat flakes stick to its broad, slightly rounded top more easily. An evergreen cauliflower, that's what it looks like to me.

Above the yard, oddly, is the street my husband Don and I live on, Armshore Drive. We are sub-road, a feature that did not appeal to us when we first saw the house five years ago. We still dislike being looked down on by passersby. The backyard of our house, which faces the Northwest Arm, more than makes up for what my husband terms our "risible" front yard. We are urban waterfront, a feature we adore and never, ever expected to experience in our lives together. There is no steel-blue water to look out onto today; our top of the Arm froze over shore to shore yesterday. Now, the snow has covered the sheen of ice with its own dull blanket. At an edge of the city, where we are, the world is a soft and peaceful place. The city keeps on humming, though, unperturbed by regular winter weather. The streets are clear, the offices and shops all open. I can buy a bottle of good wine, a pepper of any hue or a still-warm baguette

– all in ten minutes from our home. I can also fill a prescription, renew a driver's licence, see the latest independent or Hollywood film, go to an art gallery, a community theatre or a Chinese restaurant for dim sum – also in ten minutes. All this makes a city girl's heart sing.

I don't even mind about the snow. Here in Halifax it doesn't frighten me the way it did when I first moved from Vancouver to rural Cape Breton in 1997. There I used to feel so claustrophobic when the blizzards rolled in day after day in the winter. During these times, driving became A Bad Idea, and the snow piled high enough that even walking my dog, Leo, a whippet, was A Major Production Of Short Duration. The dog didn't so much walk as swim through the drifts, his stick legs translucent with the cold and his thin body covered in a fleecy coat he hated and tried to rub off. He was game, I was grumpy. I was also deeply shocked by the cold, especially when it dipped below minus twenty degrees Celsius. *We're a long way from home, Leo,* I'd say, a pseudo-echo of Dorothy's line in *The Wizard of Oz.* Some days there was no point in going anywhere. At thirty-eight years old, I had never experienced being housebound due to weather. Some mornings I'd open the curtains in our bedroom and start crying.

"Are you all right?" my startled soon-to-be husband asked the first time this happened, in November 1997.

"The snow," I choked out. "It's still here."

And he, a Maritimer by choice and passion but like me, a West Coaster by raising, understood.

"Ah, you poor mutt," he said, using a favourite term of affection, "you thought it would melt overnight, be gone by the morning – didn't you?"

I nodded miserably. To me, it felt as though the world had disappeared. How did one navigate with no green to guide them?

*No green to guide me.* My beloved Pacific coast world was extravagantly green and lush. The rain forest had been my home since I was four years old, and moved to Vancouver from Ottawa with my mother, father and three older siblings in 1963. My father, an arts showman and visionary, had accepted the position of director of the Vancouver Art Gallery. My mother, perhaps one of the most consistent intellectuals I've ever known, was farther from her books than she felt comfortable being, with the full-time care of four children, but very much game for the move. All of us settled into Vancouver life as though Ontario were a hazy dream. Life became saltwater swimming and picnicking on city beaches, camping on the North Shore mountains and at Tofino and Qualicum Beach on Vancouver Island, Chinatown feasts on Sunday evening and bicycling down to Southlands or "The Flats," a term my older sister Karin and I breathed as though exhaling magic particles into the air.

Of all improbabilities, Southlands, located in the southwestern corner of the city, minutes from where we lived, was horse country. Over a thousand horses lived on this flat and muddy land, about one hundred rurally-zoned acres in total. The area was also significantly below sea level, with deep ditches on all its roads. Its southernmost boundary ran next to the Fraser River, which, along with the life-teeming delta itself, was another fascinating and fundamental aspect to Vancouver life.

Tough, polluted, fish- and boat-filled, the Fraser was the colour of pea soup in summer and slate in the winter. Karin and I dreamed of riding our very own horses along the riverside trails that led on into the University of British Columbia's "Endowment Lands," or the protected, forested acres that still surround the university, now recognized by most as the traditional lands of the Musqueam First Nation. In early years we had to content ourselves with the occasional, expensive ride on shaggy ponies at the for-hire stables. We kept on dreaming, certain we could will a horse into our lives. Once we'd inhaled the complex and sharp smells of a barn – hay, straw, manure, animal sweat, lime, liniments and leather – we claimed them more as home than any other four-walled structure. Going to The Flats at dawn on a summer morning was an excitement we could only just endure, like every Christmas morning and birthday we'd ever known, arriving on the same rosy-skied day. Belly-hungry and soul-sated, we bicycled home, our legs latticed with bright green grass from cut summer lawns. We listened with one ear as our mother asked us to towel off the grass before stepping in the house. We washed before breakfast, but we mostly couldn't wait till our hands, clothes and hair reeked of the barn world again.

## JANUARY 9, 2011, HALIFAX, NOVA SCOTIA

This is exactly the sort of winter morning that used to alarm me so much: in just a few short hours the world has become a uniformly white place. The poor rhododendron is now squashed low with the weight of the snow and the yews are coated over, even on the sides. The snow here, as my stepson Mark once pointed out to me, generally comes down horizontally, or in a wind-crossed pattern that rivals lace for complexity. He had nothing but contempt for the more pedestrian brand of snow he lives with now, in Medicine Hat, Alberta. There the snow only comes down like a curtain, he says. Very dull and predictable.

Neither adjective could ever be applied to Nova Scotia weather. What's that expression Maritimers are so fond of? "Don't like the weather? Wait a minute or walk a mile!" Of course that would be true for weather in Atlantic Canada overall. Hurricanes, gales, blizzards, torrential, tropically warm rains, freezing rain, humidity high enough to leaden limbs and make the exteriors of toilet tanks weep determined rivers and refrigerators rust – Atlantic Canada gets it all and in no particular pattern or cycle. And Maritimers for certain love the drama, diversion and even threat of their often wild weather. They love their weather, period.

Overall, the woman from the Pacific Rain Forest loves it, too. I am not so keen on the power-outs or icy highways. But any Maritimer might say that. To themselves, if no one else. And amongst themselves, with great gusto, if the need to weather-vent came upon them. As a CFA (Come-From-Away), I try not to whinge too much. Don't want to give us a bad name. In truth, I think of myself as a Maritimer now, anyway – which feels very odd some days. How could it be otherwise, though? It's been a decade and a half of Maritime immersion. I love my adopted homeland and I've had the biggest Maritime fan of all, my husband Don, show me all that's best and beautiful about the region.

Don might have been raised in B.C., but no one remembers that. He's been a Maritimer for so long they always claim him as one of their own, proudly, too. Of course his heart will always be in Cape Breton, no matter where else we live. Cape Breton isn't a piece of geography. It's a State of the Spirit, complex and compelling.

This is what I have come to know in the past fifteen years.

## 2

# THE FIRST PHONE CALL

*TUESDAY, MAY 7, 1996, VANCOUVER, BRITISH COLUMBIA*

"Hi, Marjorie, it's Silver Donald Cameron calling from Cape Breton."

Of course! I nearly recognized his voice, but it's been quite a while since we last communicated and that was by letter, I think. He has a mellow and warm voice; I enjoyed listening to it when I did my interview with him in April 1994. My God, that was a long interview, too. We just couldn't seem to stop talking – even long after he'd answered all my questions for the profile I was writing for *Trek*, the University of British Columbia's alumni magazine. He was in B.C. on a book tour and was being profiled because he was a distinguished alumnus. I, a freelance writer and another UBC alum, had been given the assignment by the magazine's editor, who thought I'd enjoy meeting "this dynamic and versatile writer who, besides that, is a really nice guy."

I did. We met at a café in Kitsilano, on the west side of the city. The sun was surprisingly warm for a spring morning in Vancouver and the Japanese cherry trees were in full pink and celestial bloom. We sat outside, drinking coffee, both glad the other smoked cigarettes. I was 104 pounds, wore a short gold skirt with a short-sleeved gold and black blouse. He was trim, wore a navy blue

Tilley jacket, had a big moustache and wavy silver hair. Dark brown eyes, lit with humour and intelligence. Nice memories, all.

"Well, hi, Don, how are you?" I know enough now not to call him Silver or even Silver Don, as many in his home province do to indicate their respect. Silver Donald is his *nom de plume*; he took on the Cape Breton-style nickname in the 1980s to separate himself from the numerous other Donald Camerons in his Scottish-rich region and across the country. Don is what friends and family call him. I consider myself a friend now, though that might be a bit presumptuous.

The line is silent. He hasn't answered my question, *How are you?* Did he hear me? Still no response, though he's clearing his throat now. *Uh-oh* – pay attention, something's going on here. His voice sounds funny – strangled up and wounded. Bad news for sure. Oh no, this is really bad. His wife, he has lost his wife to cancer. Just a month ago, on Easter weekend. What do I say?

"I am so sorry. You told me such lovely stories about your wife – about your life in Cape Breton and all your sailing adventures together. I thought I'd get to meet Lulu."

He'd said, that day of the interview, "If you're ever down our way, please come by. We'd love to see you. I think you and Lulu would really hit it off." It was a genuine invitation, I was sure then, and am sure now. Everything he'd told me about Cape Bretoners – and his wife was a Cape Bretoner – indicated lovely open natures and welcoming ways. It would have been wonderful to visit the region and to know one person there, and then his family, to make things a bit easier for a first-timer to the Maritimes.

Lulu. I'd never heard a man speak so warmly and respectfully about his wife – and that, if I remember right, at the fifteen-year-married mark. Made my guts ache, when I compared his open admiration and love to how I was being treated by a casual boyfriend at the time. Aretha Franklin had it right, I thought – all we want is a little respect. And sunny meadows of love.

I walked away from Don that day, thinking, "Damn it, if there's one man that kind and loving out there, then there has to be two – I'll just have to find the other one." I'd even laughingly told myself that Don might have a brother – and perhaps he was available! The thought was a brief one. I am thirty-seven. Don is fifty-nine. That's a twenty-two-year age gap.

Even a younger brother would be too old for me.

I am glad you called, I hear myself saying to Silver Donald Cameron of D'Escousse. Where *is* this, anyway? He has said it is a village – how quaint! – with a population of 250 people, on an island, off another island, off the peninsular province of Nova Scotia. I've never been east of Montreal, and I can't hold all this geography in my mind. I can't imagine living in a place so small you need an atlas to find it. Not for love nor money. Besides, I love this West Coast of mine far too much to ever live somewhere else.

As I remember, Don spoke the same way about the Maritimes; he may have been raised on the West Coast but when he left at age twenty-seven, he really left – he doesn't miss it at all. We are lucky, Don and I, to know where our hearts' homes are.

Astonishingly, we have talked for over an hour. For the last ten minutes, his voice has been going flatter and softer. He's heartbroken and tired, from all the demands and tasks a death brings to a family, that's obvious – but it's also past midnight his time. Time to wrap up.

"I'd like to send you a couple of my books – would you like that?" He sounds shy, as though I might actually say no to such a kind suggestion. Books from an author of his stature? Yes, please!

"Oh, thank you! I'd love that. Perhaps the one about the fishermen's strike that you mentioned – Everett something?"

"*The Education of Everett Richardson*. Yeah, with your expertise in fisheries, I think you'd like that. I'll send on a book of personal essays, too – there are some hard ones in there, like the essay about your sister Karin. That's so great you won for that one."

The win he's referring to is a National Magazine Award in 1994. I hadn't bragged about that – even though a part of me still can't believe it – he had brought up the subject and we'd talked about it at length, mostly about the writerly aspects of making family tragedy into readable, worthwhile prose. In this case, my essay, through a complicated set of circumstances, had ultimately been published in *Saturday Night* magazine as a companion piece with another essay written by my oldest sister, writer and poet Zoë Landale. The two of us had written about a third sibling, our sister Karin Simmins. The oddest part about all this was that neither Zoë nor I knew the other was writing about Karin at the same time – and this after almost twenty years had passed since her death. Don had actually heard the interview Zoë and I had done for CBC Radio the week before the win; it was just prior to the same week I had met him, so he had warmly wished me all good luck in the competition and had then written me a brief note when the win transpired. The note was a classy touch, I'd thought at the time.

"I haven't read the piece," he is saying. He laughs, "Hard to get a copy of *Saturday Night* or much else where I live! Could you send me a copy? It's about a sister of yours – right? Her name is –?"

"– was, her name was Karin."

I will send him my essay on Karin, the one everyone wants to read. I'll send him another one too, one that I wrote *for* her, not *about* her.

## TRIPS FROM THERE TO HERE
### VANCOUVER, BRITISH COLUMBIA, 1993

When I think about Karin, I remember bacon and marmalade sandwiches and chocolate milk, the kind that comes out of the carton thick and sweet. And fried pork chops and baked potatoes with sour cream, her favourite dinner, back in the days when she was allowed to eat with us. I don't remember who banished her from the dinner table or when, but I remember why.

Throwing up. Anything that went down when she was stoned came flying back up within minutes. We tolerated this vomiting, even accommodated it: we always made sure she had the outside chair in our kitchen nook. That way, when she felt sick, she could run to the bathroom without tripping all over us. Sometimes she wasn't fast enough to make it to the bathroom. The back door would smash open and we'd hear food splatter onto the cement walkway below the veranda. We kept a garden hose coiled at the side of the house.

First memories of my sister always come with the sound of raised voices and the feeling of dread in my stomach. I used to run to the bathroom upstairs, the farthest corner away from the noise. I'd turn on the tap and hum as I brushed my teeth, trying to block out the yells from downstairs. I knew she wouldn't hurt me – I was too young to have anything she wanted – but she hurt the others with a bewildering and relentless accuracy. I couldn't stand watching the fights and I couldn't prevent them, so I created my own territory with her, the safest one I could think of: sister as shadow. I decided to be friends with her, to move beside her, where I could keep her in my peripheral vision.

Karin went through a magician phase; maybe sorceress is a better word. She used to put on performances in her incense-sweet bedroom in the basement. She had special clothes for these occasions, harem pants and gauzy scarfs that she wrapped around her red-gold hair. Sometimes she would make things disappear and other times she'd open cupboard doors just by looking at them. A neighbour who watched one of these shows couldn't resist trying to destroy Karin's illusions.

"Look," she said, "she's using a string to pull the door open! I can see it, can't you?"

Karin's eyes searched the darkened room, looking for mine. Speak up. Guard the magic.

"Mrs. Williams, you're wrong. There's no string. This is real magic." I glared at her. The show concluded to loud applause.

Cats loved Karin, loved the way she rubbed their wet noses and hypnotized them with soft words and fishy treats. Some days I felt like a cat, gut-happy and mind-stroked with gentle words and promises. As long as I protected her – accepted her choices and rules – the anger never came my way. I didn't know how else to protect myself.

We used to play horses out in the backyard. We'd take our horse collection – plastic and china figures – and set up a farm in the rock garden. Usually we chose the spot where the water faucet was hidden by a low, thick azalea bush. There were flat rocks beneath the faucet. When it rained, or when the faucet was left on a steady drip, the rocks held a shallow pool of water. We called this the pond and took the horses to swim there. I could play for hours, but Karin eventually got bored and the game would end with a ritualistic drowning of the horses. Hands that had moments earlier created bridles out of elastic bands and gently braided manes and tails would now seize the small animals and shove their heads under the water, making them gurgle and scream. I could sense the mood change, could see impatience in the movement of her fingers – but the vibrancy of her imagination was irresistible. In the garden of our make-believe world, death was a temporary condition; I knew I would play with her again the next day, when the sorceress pulled us up from the chill waters to start a new game.

Karin's eyes were dark blue, with a silver star around the iris. She plucked her eyebrows thin and wore heavy eyeliner. Pale skin, with a few freckles scattered over a finely shaped nose. Her stride was short, almost bouncy. In nearly all of her photographs she has her head tilted to one side – her expression a strange blend of coyness and misery.

I don't remember when her blue eyes started going grey every day. Around the same time she started taking her meals in the TV room. It was a relief to eat quiet dinners; I even started enjoying spaghetti again. But I was uneasy with the separation – and disliked cutting her off from the rest of the family. The non-offenders would exchange news of the day, pass the butter, salt and pepper around the table, and I'd be worrying if she wanted more food, or if she'd nodded out over her plate. As soon as I could I'd join her in the den. We'd watch TV together, sprawled out on the couch, me leaning on her side with a pillow underneath my elbow. Her cigarette ash would burn longer and longer and without thinking I'd reach over and bump her arm over the ashtray.

"Karin, watch your smoke."

We started to find burn holes everywhere. The couch, the pillowcases, the bedsheets. She always seemed to wake up just before the smoke turned to flames.

Karin kept her methadone bottles in the refrigerator. She lined them up tidily, on the right-hand side of the door, nestled in with the Velveeta cheese. The methadone was mixed with orange juice, which masked the bitter taste a little bit. Karin told me never to touch them. But I did. I was curious about those white-capped bottles, even jealous of their daily importance. After everyone was asleep I'd sneak down to the kitchen and pull a bottle out. Sometimes I'd just smell the stuff, and wonder what she felt like when she drank it. One night I took a tiny slurp, then, terrified she'd know I had tried it, I filled the missing half-inch with water and ran back to bed. I lay awake a long time, wondering when I'd get smashed. I fell asleep with a trace of orange-sweet drug juice on my lips.

The year we bought Coqeyn, I recorded the event in my journal: "Over the weekend we bought a horse. He is an Arabian and Karin and I are going to look after it." Every twelve-year-old girl's dream come true. A living, breathing horse, to ride and love.

Coqeyn scared me. Mostly because I was sure we'd lose him, the moment our reflection in his purple-brown eyes became steady. Vet bills, board bills, and my mother teaching day school and night school to provide for us. I'd watch Mum disappear into her bedroom for a twenty-minute rest before dinner and hate the horse for filling the house with dragging steps and exhaustion. But Coqeyn was going to save the day: he was going to make Karin permanently straight and functioning. Like magic.

Karin's all-time straight record in seven years was three months. Straight from heroin and barbiturates. She drank the methadone every day, although at one point she weaned herself down to a quarter of a bottle, selling the other three-quarters to buy things for the horse. The endless supply of methadone came from the Narcotics Addiction Foundation, on Broadway at Oak, where we went once a week. On the bus down there Karin would drink Coke, to fill her bladder for the sample she had to give to the doctors. Some days her bladder wouldn't cooperate. She'd park herself by the water fountain in the foundation's foyer and drink until the twinge in her gut felt certain.

"Okay, I'm ready." I'd watch her disappear into the bathroom, followed by a woman in a white lab coat. Minutes later, she'd return, smiling and giggling, jerking her thumb at the full sample bottle carried by the nurse: "Success!" Then she'd line up with the other junkies to get her methadone for the week. They always made her drink a cup of methadone before she left. She'd throw back her head, toss the liquid down, and make a major production of swallowing it. Actually, she didn't swallow any, but kept it in her mouth until we left the building from the back entrance. If I felt like teasing her, I'd poke her in the ribs, trying to make her laugh and spit the liquid out of her chipmunk cheeks. She'd shake her head, look furious, but I knew it was like the horses in the pond – no permanent damage done.

In the lane behind the foundation she'd take out one of her bottles and spit the methadone into it. She spat it out fast, discreet; you'd think she was stopping to cough and delicately wipe her mouth. We'd walk another half-block and sell the topped-up bottle to the first junkie with cash.

Karin loved Coqeyn as much as she loved smack. We groomed our horse, one on either side, until our arms ached. We read horse magazines and made plans to truck Coqeyn into the Interior, where we could go for long rides into the mountains. He would be an endurance horse, a jumper, a hunter – he was going to do it all and we were going to have a roomful of ribbons and trophies to gloat over. We took riding lessons, sold methadone, and bought expensive tack. Summer 1972: Jethro Tull (*Thick as a Brick*), paisley T-shirts, Export A cigarettes, and the barn, every day, all day.

There were triumphs in those years. The first time we won a ribbon at a recognized show I cried so hard I could hardly see where I was going as I ran over the bumpy hogfuel to meet Karin coming out of the ring.

"It's only a sixth place, Marjorie," she protested as I grabbed onto her gloved hand and squeezed it hard.

"But a ribbon, Karin! A rosette!"

She dismounted, leaned against Coqeyn's sweat-darkened shoulder. "Next time we'll do better."

Doing better. The words throbbed under our skins as the boundaries between us blurred. Doing better this week, only lied once about no bombers in the house. Found a rainbow assortment in her jewellery box, flushed them down the toilet. Doing better, though, no clouds in her eyes for three days. Relax, play the twin game: Levi jeans, blue ski jackets, black boots, velvet hunt caps, long hair in braids. Walk close, shoulders touching, steps synchronized. No one can tell us apart. You protect me and I'll protect you.

These periods – the quiet, symbiotic ones – vanished. One week we were inseparable; the next I was a Siamese twin slowly ripping my body away from hers. We all tried to keep out of her way, to hide from the cruel taunts, the thievery, the broken dishes. My brother hid by going out with his friends; he spent nearly all his time at parties or in bars and pool halls. I used to ask him, as he was leaving, where he was going. The fringes on his leather jacket would swing as he shrugged his shoulders. "Out," he'd say, "going out." The door would slam behind him and I'd be left standing in the hallway, wondering where I could go. In six more months I would seek out all of Geoffrey's haunts and claim them as my own, but before then I spent many evenings walking around the back lanes behind our house.

Sometimes she'd still be up when I returned.

"Where have you been? I'm making a milkshake, would you like some?" Maybe she felt guilty or ashamed; maybe she just wanted to keep me on her side. I'd watch her pour the milkshake and accept the glass timidly. We'd go to the TV room and before I had a sip from my glass I'd wait, knowing she'd either spill hers or demand the rest of mine.

Her eyes and her moods were dead giveaways. Easy to know when she was high. When she got really affectionate, I knew it would be a back-lane night.

"Oh, Marjorie, I feel so good today. I'm so glad we're friends, aren't you? I love you, little sister, I love you so much." Words like those coiled every muscle in my body for flight. Karin's love always careened into anger.

Eventually even the horse wasn't safe. When Karin started coming to the barn stoned, I knew that I had to complete my separation from her. If I didn't, I'd find myself explaining not just a broken dish or a missing wallet, but a death.

The final break came. I was in the feed room, mixing up a steaming bran mash. Karin burst in the door, eyes as wide as they could be when she was that high. Her face was white and sweaty, her words so slurred that at first I couldn't make out what she was saying.

"Come quick. It's in his stall, the cigarette, right by the door, I can't find it, hurry, hurry – come!"

He's gonna burn. He's gonna rear up in a box of flames and cook like a pig in a bonfire. Fear for Coqeyn made my heart lurch, but stronger than the fear was the pattern of hiding Karin's mistakes. No one would know what had happened, not if I moved quickly. I wanted to hit that pasty, out-of-focus face, but I just told her to get a wheelbarrow and start shovelling out the stall. I led Coqeyn out, tied him to a post. Stepped back inside the stall and glanced back over my shoulder to see who could see me. No one around. I tipped over the three-foot-high water bucket in the corner where she said she'd dropped the cigarette. All this time Karin was babbling and weaving, getting in my way. My hands, sticky with warm molasses, shook so much I could barely hold the shovel.

"Get out of my way. Get the fuck out of here." New and raw words I hurled at her, words that had nothing to do with the cigarette and a lot to do with the twin feeling its air supply being choked off. Breathe, little sister, breathe hard and fast.

Her expression was terrifying – dead straight and stoned to the limit. Of all her unusual abilities, this was the one that frightened me most. While anyone else would have fallen flat with the amount of chemicals she pumped into her body, small Karin staggered on, even casting aside, for a few minutes, the total effect of the drugs she had taken. "Thought I was a goner, sister/brother dear?" she'd sneer at Geoffrey and me, when we'd crouch beside her, deciding whether or not to call an ambulance. "Not yet, motherfuckers."

I concentrated on cleaning out the stall. By now I wasn't even scared about the cigarette. More was coming. Every hair standing up on my arms was preparing me for it.

When I came back from soaking the chips with water I found Karin tightening the girth on Coqeyn's saddle. The bridle was already on.

"What are you doing?" I kept my voice low and prayed she couldn't hear the pleading note beneath it.

"Gonna ride in the ring." As she spoke she lost her balance and caught at the bridle to steady herself. Coqeyn, jabbed in the mouth from this motion, threw up his head and took several quick steps backwards. "Stand still, you bastard." She kneed him hard under the girth.

"Stop it!" I was shouting now, didn't care who heard me. "Leave him alone."

"Why? This bother you?" she asked, eyes for one instant clear and sober. "Watch, it gets better."

She took the bridle in both hands and jerked it down with all her weight. I could feel that iron cut down as though the bit were in my own mouth. I sucked in cold night air and howled. Coqeyn lunged, I lunged, Karin laughed. I pushed her down onto the tarmac and felt her rise up against my arms strong as a tidal wave. Fluid strength, like water all around us, and me twisting, kicking, punching to keep my head from going under.

I lost the fight. And I never walked shoulder to shoulder with Karin again.

That autumn I started grade nine. School was something that passed between hours of wondering whether Karin had died that day. Her eyes looked like grey cauliflowers now, with hardly any colour in them at all. She overdosed so many times that I got used to seeing her face blue. I distanced myself from my hands when they slapped the breath into her. She hurt herself, horribly, when she was stoned – gashes, bruises – but I didn't help her any more. I ate my meals in the kitchen with the rest of the family and afterwards I retreated to my room.

One morning I came downstairs and found her passed out, with her eyes open, in the chair beside the front door. I stepped close to her, to see if she was breathing. It was a quarter to nine; if I didn't hurry, I'd be late for school. I couldn't bring myself to touch her. I imagined she was a corpse that would suddenly reach out and crush my body into the deathland behind those unblinking eyes. Geoffrey walked into the hall, saw me staring at her slumped figure.

"She alive?"

"I can't tell, I think so. Wouldn't her eyes be closed if she was dead?"

"Maybe, don't know. Let's get out of here."

We walked up Dunbar Street towards the bus loop. Geoffrey's strides were long and fast; I took two for each one of his. Suddenly aware of our mismatched steps, he slowed down, until our shoulders brushed together. He reached into his jacket pocket and took out a Bar Six chocolate bar.

"Want some?"

"Yeah, sure."

Karin died a year later, in a room at the Blue Boy hotel. On Christmas Day. Unlike the china and plastic horses, she would stay dead.

I didn't ride for about eight years. Barns, with their cold cement floors and draughty corridors, felt like tombs. The smell of molasses made me sick. And when I saw young women with long hair and blue ski jackets walking close together, I'd stretch out my arms and feel oceans of empty air on either side of my body.

My hair is short now. I wear a purple and black Gore-Tex jacket when I ride in the rain. Black leather chaps, too; Karin would have loved them. Since my sister died, I have travelled in Europe, Canada, the United States, and the West Indies. I have lived on boats, in downtown high-rises. I went to university and worked, as a waitress, a driver, an editor. Men, for days and daze, and two, loved unconditionally. I kissed/kiss them, remembering Karin's precise explanation of the perfect kiss.

Last year I even dated a brother of one of her lovers. I met him, in one of those small-world situations, and wanted to be near him, because his brother had loved Karin. A tall and strange order to fill, and he only five feet eight inches, with a mind more focused on gains than losses.

"Yeah," he said, "Kevin did heroin, but he's been clean for years. Your sister didn't make it, eh?"

"Where was your brother when Karin died?" (First date, the Holiday Inn on Broadway, him figuring out my income tax return, me scanning his face for one flicker of shared memory.)

"I don't know. Maybe they weren't friends any more. Besides, drugs weren't really a problem for Kevin. He hasn't used in years. He's married now, has a kid, and works as an actor – very talented. Why are you so hung up on the past?"

"He wasn't at her memorial service." (Only saw Lana, ward-of-the-state Lana, crying and gibbering with fear because Karin was the smart one and why were her ashes in an urn when all the dummies were still living?)

"Really? I wouldn't know. Now listen, do you want to get some money back – or a lot of money back?"

I wanted to sleep beside him, reach out for a dream fragment of his brother, my sister. I wanted to remember, for a moment, soft rubber tied around my fourteen-year-old arm and the sharp press of an empty needle against a blue, untravelled vein. Karin? Where do I stick this thing? Right in the vein? Or beside it, or under it, or in any part of my arm that is willing? Does the needle have to have heroin in it, or will water from the basement sink give me a rush?

Couldn't do it – needles belonged to Karin. I watched her, though, and tied her arm when I couldn't stand her bad moods any more. She wore a lingering perfume called Omar's Delight, which she bought from a store on 4th Avenue. She smelled sweet, as I leaned close to watch her perfect aim with the needle.

## Escape Of The Smallest Angel
### – For Karin Francesca Simmins –
### Vancouver, British Columbia, 1995

My mother and I decorated our Christmas tree last night. We had nearly finished – the boughs were crowded with birds, bulbs and lights – when Mum turned to me with a broken ornament in her hands.

"We don't need this one, do we?" she asked, her hands cupped around a small silver globe with an angel inside.

"Yes!" I hurried across the room and took the decoration from my mother's outstretched hands. "That one has to go up." I placed it on a branch near the top of the tree, then stepped back, to make sure the angel could be seen through the shimmering strands of icicles. Visible and secure, the angel spun gently within its cage. Then I answered the question in my mother's eyes.

"Don't you remember the story of the smallest angel?"

Christmas morning, 1964. Dad and Mum still asleep, and me waking my brother and two sisters in the pre-dawn darkness. We sit cross-legged on my oldest sister's bed and open our bulging stockings. Candy canes, chocolates, small gifts wrapped in bright tissue paper and at the toe of the stocking, as always, a Mandarin orange, thin-skinned and sweet. The basement stairs creak as we make our way up to the living room, where the lights of the tree cast blurred reflections on a rain-streaked window. The room is cold – no heat on yet – but we are warm in our cotton pyjamas and wool socks. We circle around the tree and begin poking and shaking the piles of gifts underneath it. We have an hour to go before we can wake our parents. Zoë goes back to bed. Geoffrey goes to the kitchen to find some breakfast. Karin and I stay by the tree.

"Can you tell me a Christmas story?"

Karin nods, her waist-long hair streaked with red and gold from the lights above our heads. I want to reach out and touch those shining waves, but the story has begun; I must be quiet and still. Karin points to a branch on the tree where three angels are placed. One holds a lantern, one holds a songbook and one is encased in a silver cage.

"In the time of never and always, there were three angels who lived in the land of mortals. They were sisters and longed to go to their true home, the place of clouds and music. Each day they asked the king of angels when they could return home and each day the king answered them: 'Not until the smallest angel can fly free, then you will all be free.'

"But the smallest angel lived in a cage that did not have a door. Her sisters could not free her, no matter how hard they tried to break the silver walls. The smallest angel cried and cried. She shook the bars of her cage and tried to squeeze through the narrow spaces, but she could not escape. She and her sisters never returned to the place of clouds and music."

Karin reaches out to the shining ornament and gently pushes the cage so it rocks on the branch. Suspended on a string, the angel sways back and forth within its narrow world. Beside her, the two sisters are motionless. But I can hear the melody of the harp and the high keen of angel voices on a dark Christmas morning.

I do not say anything when Karin gets up to find another Mandarin orange. I sit under the glowing lights and feel the sharp fragrance of Douglas fir press against my nose. The smallest angel floats down from her branch and slips into the sleeve of my pyjamas. Down we go to the basement, where the tool cupboard is jammed with nails, screwdrivers and hammers.

An hour later the heat registers in the living room are blasting up warm air and the floor is covered with scrunched paper and ribbon. Books, clothes and toys are scattered throughout the room. At the moment my teeth settle onto a bite of cinnamon toast, my brother asks the question I had prayed no one would ask.

"Who broke the angel's cage?"

Silence, while everyone looks to the branch where the smallest angel hangs. Sure enough, the cage enclosing the angel is broken, although the angel herself is unharmed and twirls within her imperfect casing. A gust of heat comes up the wall and turns the ornament toward the window, hiding the jagged opening from our eyes.

"Maybe the dog got it," I suggest. Accusing faces focus on our German shepherd puppy, Lorenzo, who is busily chewing a scrap of wood from the fireplace. Feeling the weight of our attention, he stops and cocks his head to one side, a worried expression in his eyes. Oh, no, I think, this isn't right, either.

"Maybe it just fell down by itself," I say. "Besides, it doesn't matter if the cage is broken, the angel looks fine." I take another bite of toast, wishing I could hear the sound of angel voices now, to guide my inexpert lies.

Karin glances at me. She is smiling and trying not to laugh. Her eyes turn up to the smallest angel.

"I agree, she looks fine. Who cares if the cage is broken?"

Christmas, 1993. The smallest angel and her sisters are together on our tree. A short visit back to the land of mortals, from the time of never and always.

*3*

# THE SECOND PHONE CALL

*FRIDAY, MAY 10, 1996, VANCOUVER, BRITISH COLUMBIA*

I am embarrassed to the tips of all my extremities, can feel what must be my hair follicles blushing – and am enjoying every squirming moment. Don has said so many kind things about my essay on my sister Karin that I've lost track of the thank yous I've said back to him. He also just *gets it* – gets the passion and pain of family love, gets its hopeless, helpless forms, and gets Karin's vast, permanent effect on all our lives. *Her death was only the beginning of a new way of living with her.*

"Thank you," I say one last time firmly and deliberately. "It means so much to me to have a writer as distinguished as you are understand what I was trying to say."

"No," he corrects me, "what you *did* say – no trying about it! It's a fabulous story. Small wonder you got a national magazine award for it. You are very obviously not just a fisheries reporter. Though I think it's great you do that!"

*I could never tell you why I am a fisheries reporter ... I don't think I could, anyway ...*

Don has four national magazine wins to his credit; I know that from the research I did on him for the profile. It's all a bit intimidating to think about sometimes. There doesn't appear to be any sort of writing he hasn't done and done well. I am only five years into this writing business. I am primarily a freelance commercial and sport fisheries reporter; as such, I don't exactly garner a lot of attention and praise from literary circles. He's right, though; I do write first-person essays and work hard to be known for more than what I term "straight," as in straight-ahead, rule-bound, journalism. *The Vancouver Sun* has been regularly publishing my essays for years. I missed having "Escape of the Smallest Angel," the second essay I sent Don, published by a matter of days. I'd sent it in to *The Saturday Review*'s editor, Max Wyman, just a bit too late for a Christmastime publication. Every freelance writer in Vancouver fights to get in Wyman's "magazine," a weekend insert published in *The Vancouver Sun.* Dad knew Wyman in post-Vancouver Art Gallery years, when Dad worked as a freelance arts reviewer for Vancouver's other daily, *The Province.* Wyman told me that when he saw my surname on the first essay I sent in, he said to himself, *Simmins? Richard Simmins' daughter?* I like to think curiosity made Wyman decide to read the essay and thereafter, the writing did what it was supposed to do.

"So, you haven't published 'Escape of the Smallest Angel' yet – is that what you said?" asks Don.

"No, I missed the Christmas deadline by a day, that's what Max Wyman told me."

"Oh, you'll sell it for sure next year. Doesn't have to be for a Christmas issue, either, I don't think." He pauses, then says wonderingly, "She really was a sorceress, wasn't she?"

He understands, I think, that I miss that. I miss magic in my life. Once upon a time, Karin's magic didn't hurt people. That's the only kind of magic I am interested in. Creative, not destructive.

"Would you send me some more of your essays?" Don asks. "I'd really enjoy that. What about the Valentine's Day essay – that sounded hilarious."

My stomach flip-flops with nerves at the request. I am silent a moment, one thought tumbling fast to the next: *Oh God, I can't send the lovelorn ones – can I? Does this nice man need to know right away about my personal failures? Writers, we share the most intimate details with a faceless world – but hold back face to face – or even writer to writer sometimes.* I take a deep breath. *I'll chance it. He seems kind. God knows he wasn't born yesterday.* I answer: "Sure, I can do that. I'll pop some in the mail tomorrow."

I am thirty-seven years old and I have been mostly single for seven years. I hate almost every aspect of being single. For me this has meant dreadfully painful mismatches, loneliness and, above all, fear that my deep longing for children will ultimately and perversely lead to a childless life. *No, that won't happen.* I need my own family as much as I need air. I spent a decade with one man – a commercial fisherman I literally loved on sight when he ran down the beach in the Queen Charlotte Islands to meet me, and four passionate and disturbing years with another man, who turned out to be a mirage. The worst kind of magic, that one; nothing was indeed as it first seemed. More than anything, I find being single confusing and completely at odds with my two-is-better nature. How can I possibly be alone – after all the heartfelt investments of a decade and a half? I've made mistakes, plenty. But I've always known how to love. This life of mine is already entirely different than anything I imagined as a girl. If the trend continues, I can't imagine what Fate has up her sleeve for me.

Ah, Fate – I am so tired of being alone. Can't you send me someone to love?

# 4

## SINGLE IN THE 1990S

### LOOKING FOR HEART
#### VANCOUVER, BRITISH COLUMBIA, 1994

"Now, *you* I could make love to," says a radiant voice somewhere near my right shoulder. Before I turn I have already guessed at the age, temperament and alcohol consumption of the speaker. The guesses send immediate waves of reassurance along the surface of my skin: young, cheerful, half-cut but not about to fall over. Harmless.

I take two steps to the left, then look up to the ship-to-shore grin of a boy-faced man dressed in denim and flannel. Rude replies dance on the underside of my tongue, but the word that does find the air surprises both of us.

"Pipsqueak."

The top half of his over-six-foot frame bends over in laughter. "I'm not a pipsqueak," he protests when he straightens up again, "and besides, I'm told that women like the aggressive approach."

The bar's busy tonight, especially down this end, where the pool tables are ringed by players and observers. Down the other end, the band plays on gamely, despite an empty dance floor and the competing clash of Friday night voices. An undemanding second set, only an hour away from midnight enthusiasm and hoarse commands for "Bob Seger, rock 'n' roll!" For now, mournful wisps of a Roy Orbison tune curl around clinking glasses and the steady ring from the cash register. I place a loonie on the edge of the closest pool table, and decide to ignore Pipsqueak.

The first time I came here by myself I was so nervous I made a beeline for the bathroom and didn't emerge for ten minutes. I looked for courage in the bathroom mirror, found wide eyes instead. The reflection spoke to me.

"Rough and tough bar – what do you think you're doing, arriving on your own?"

*Want to relax, shoot some pool.*

"But why here?"

*Close to the ocean, close to home. Small. A Cheers clone, where everyone seems to know everyone else. Like the talk too, of fish, lumber, working long days and more of those days to come, but we'll get by.*

"You should have a guy friend with you, or a girlfriend."

*Don't want to be with either tonight. Enjoy my own company. What's wrong with that?*

"So why are you so keyed up?"

*Good question.*

I held my clammy hands under a jet of warm water. Tense, release. As my fingers moved, the heat seemed to spread up my arms and into my shoulders. No fear then, only a growing certainty that in this place, or wherever else I might choose to go alone, my intuition and good sense would keep me safe. No matter what the situation, I decided, the right words and right actions would come to me. I dried my hands and walked back out to the bar with my head high and back straight.

And who says faith isn't rewarded? Met my first "spare brother" that night three years ago. Tall, short, shy or lively, I can now spot spare brother from a mile away. Something about an easiness to the set of chin, line of jaw, cross of arms. A gentle spacing between shoulder blades. Sharp-eyed panthers, they'd step between me and trouble in a moment. I've never had to ask for this intervention. But I could. No price for protection, either.

There are "spare sisters" in here, too. Stories shared of where we've been and where we're going: histories, dreams, strategies. Their energy and sassiness spills onto me – makes our toes tap and hands circle in the air. So many separate journeys, different choices made. Comfort in the sharing.

Pipsqueak is telling me his name. My mind refuses to register it, as I've already christened him satisfactorily and thought the conversation was finished. Apparently not. The word "aggressive" passes my ears again.

"Who told you women like aggressive men?"

"My friend."

"Guy or a woman?"

"Guy."

"Well, he's wrong. Dead wrong." Memory-touch of water on my hands, the washing away of imagined threat, a renewal of belief in self-care. An acceptance of danger in this world; a rejection of its power over me. Firm conviction that men and women want to get along, need one another as friends, lovers and providers of emotional sanctuary. Brothers and sisters, who keep no tally of favours offered or received.

A moment of quiet while Pip debates a final point in support of an aggressive stance.

"Well," he says finally, "it works for my friend."

"Is it working for you?"

"Not really ..." He looks dejected and tired, but if it's my turn to be a spare sister, then I'm going to see it through to the end.

"What do you believe?"

"Money, women want guys with money."

Where do these ideas come from? Did a woman actually say this to him? Or was it the dreaded "friend" again? This perception, in my experience, is so far off base that I don't know what to say. Disturbing to hear from such a young man. Got to change the focus somehow. Just one or two sentences that he might remember tomorrow morning, foggy head and all.

"Trust me, it's not money, it's heart. Women want guys with big hearts. Got to go now, my loonie's up." No answer to this, only a shrug of shoulders and solo hiccup. One last thing to say to him.

"Hey, Pip, you're not driving, are you?" He shakes his head. As I move away he reaches out and tugs on the sleeve of my shirt.

"You really are good-looking," he says, "for someone your age."

Can't hit a brother, can I?

## EYES OF A STRANGER
### VANCOUVER, BRITISH COLUMBIA, VALENTINE'S DAY, 1993

I tell my friends I am a novice at the Convent of the Immaculate Conception – the code phrase for being single in the '90s. I have not taken my final vows, but on some days the words ring sweet in my ears. In the midst of contemplating a life of chastity and virtue, however, a good friend sets me up on a blind date.

"Do you know this man?" I ask, a bit nervous and a lot curious.

"Not exactly," she says brightly. "But I'm told he's very nice."

"Nice," I echo, "something like a digestive biscuit, to be taken with tea?"

"Come on," she says. "Where's your sense of adventure?"

My sense of adventure ran screaming to the convent doors when the last man I dated extolled the virtues of the Walton Family and the joys of spiritual sex. I thought he was joking, until he explained that kissing was reserved for the celebration of the twenty-fifth wedding anniversary and that single beds prevented divorce. These sentiments were followed by the incomprehensible statement that he wished to father four children. I wished him luck – and fled.

I remind my friend of this episode.

"Lightning never strikes twice," she giggles. "This man is totally different. He's as close to your checklist as we've seen in a long time."

"I'm listening."

"Over thirty and under fifty."

"Uh-huh. What else?"

"Never married. No dependents. Intelligent. Works hard. Oh, yeah, and get this, he even writes."

"He writes? What kind of stuff?"

"Don't know. You'll have to find out."

"So how do you know him?"

"Friend of a friend."

"And of course the friend is reliable … ?"

"Oh, ye of little faith …"

Saturday night arrives. I have changed my clothes six times and still feel as though I'm wearing the wrong thing, which at this point is warm, all black and comfortable. I sit in the overstuffed chair in my living room, gripping my journal and blowing smoke rings.

Oh God, cigarettes. He'll be a non-smoker from Hell who turns on his heel when I ask for a light. Before we've even exchanged astrological signs, he'll tell me he exited his ten-year relationship because she was a puffer.

The doorbell rings. My dog flies to the door. I consider, briefly, allowing the dog to jump up and cover this stranger in white hairs and sloppy canine kisses. No, I think, hauling on Leo's collar, I will be nice ... and demure ... and witty ... and charming ... the man won't believe his good luck.

The blind date is tall, dark-haired, has lovely bright eyes and is dressed in an immaculate navy blue suit. I realize, the moment I open the door, that I am totally underdressed and am not speaking any language known to humankind – blatherspeak, disguised as I'm-normal-hope-you-are-please-come-in. He seems to understand the drift of my babble. Yes, he has stepped into the house and now sits down on the couch. The dog, despite my best efforts, is using him as a trampoline. Have I shaken his hand yet? No, I haven't. Perhaps I should before I ask him if he likes dogs/horses/cats/croissants on Sunday morning.

During those first awkward moments of meeting, I see my house through the stranger's eyes. Stereo, records, books, guitars, paintings, a foot-high pile of newspapers set by the fireplace, animal toys strewn on the carpet. I am fully dressed and yet I feel bare, set against the intimate environment of my home. I walk to the hall closet, pull out my coat. Time to leave.

We're in his car now, heading out to a nearby restaurant for an after-dinner drink. The conversation is proceeding, if not flowing; he asks questions about my work, I ask questions about his. It is determined that I am a writer and that he sells Saturns, the "safest car on the road." In this same car we drive to the village of Steveston. By the time we walk to the restaurant door, my feet are soaked from the slushy remnants of last weekend's snowstorm. Not only do I feel too casually dressed, I also wish I'd worn waterproof boots. Carry on.

And then the moment I'd been dreading: "Will that be smoking or non-smoking?"

I say nothing, uncertain if this question will begin or finish the evening. The silence extends, until the waiter makes an executive decision.

"I think the lady would like smoking, sir," he says and leads us to a window table overlooking the Fraser. At last, I feel comfortable: no matter into which unknown territory we stray, I can always touch home in the familiar sight of fishing boats and the river.

And the territory is not so unusual. We talk about writing, commercial fishing, university, family, politics and hobbies. And then, when my second Spanish coffee and his second glass of wine arrive, we become a little braver and discuss the people who affected our lives most.

But the sentences are short, the explanations ludicrous: without the trust, there cannot be detail. And for some reason, this woman does not trust this man and vice versa. We become edgy and every few minutes, one of us fires a direct shot – but the deflections are agile, grudgingly admired by the archer of the moment.

Why are you this, why am I that, while the lights on the water shine and the music from the twelve-string guitar blends with evasions and half-truths.

Most of all I am confused that the man sitting across the table from me is not someone I know well or love. He's nice, I'm nice, but we are not known to one another, nor will we be, despite the efforts of mutual friends. When I look up to his face I expect to see the blue eyes I loved for four years or the tawny gold eyes I loved for nine – and instead I see a stranger who is equally surprised to see a woman with green eyes looking at him.

Midnight. He drives me home and we exchange "goodnight" and "nice to meet you." I consider shaking his hand again, but it's not necessary: this is our first and last meeting.

In the morning, there is the phone call to make to my friend, who is happily anticipating good news – or at the very least, a good story.

"Not a kindred spirit?" she asks, when I try to explain how the only reflection of light I saw was on the waters of the Fraser. "But he said he writes – does he?"

"He's *thinking* about writing. Has been, for some years."

Back to quiet thoughts and the rhythm of my own writing. I light a candle, put on a record and call my dog to join me on the chair. I am warm and comfortable. I am also smiling and thinking that the convent's not so bad a place – at this point in time.

One day a door will swing open, and I'll see a face I know well and eyes I love, long before I stretch out a hand in greeting. I'll be wearing the right clothes, the right shoes and the cigarettes will be discarded, along with the rest of my worry beads. As for the stranger, his heart is full of river songs, and he has just decided that green eyes are irresistible.

## Meeting The Challenge
### Vancouver, British Columbia, 1995

I was hoping he'd wait, at least for a few minutes, but no such luck. I have only enough time to close my eyes against the splash of jade waters as my friend dives from the wharf into the lake. Eyes open again, I see an expression of smiling challenge rise above the surface. Can't very well stand here, a vertical testament to cowardice ...

The water is an icy club against my heart. The blow spreads along the length of my body, leaving me gasping with shock of cold, stun of movement. Head up now, arms a blurred circle of water-cut to wharf-edge. Ladder, climb, wood under my feet again. I feel electric, jubilant. Been a while, it seems, since this rounded, physical connection to the elements.

After the swim we sit on opposite sides of the picnic table set above the lake shore. The sun is warm, if not hot, and there is no immediate need to change into dry clothes. From my purse I find a brush and pull it squeakily through my dripping hair.

Suddenly shy, I wonder if my non-waterproof mascara has left me looking like a raccoon. A recreational hazard that hardly matters and yet I dab a towel edge under my eyes, take a self-absorbed moment to think about the short time I have known this man.

We met several months ago, in a business context. Worked together for two days, exchanged phone numbers, said we'd keep in contact. Similar life experiences, mutual acquaintances, easy conversation – the term "stranger" never seemed to enter into the equation. The word "friend" did, before I knew his surname. Which is why I called him, out of the blue yesterday morning, saying I had to see green today.

"You know how it is," I laughed over the telephone from my home in Richmond to his home near Squamish. "Sometimes you just have to get away from the concrete. Need the green of forest all around. So, you free for a picnic?"

Despite the laughter, there's an edge to my voice I'm hoping he can't hear. I need the comfort of a vibrant coastal world and I also need platonic, emotionally undemanding company.

"Sure, come on up."

"Oh, one other thing. Got a dog. Very cute, not hairy." He does like dogs, doesn't he? Can't go anywhere without my canine sidekick.

"Great, bring him along."

Of course he likes dogs, wouldn't be a kindred spirit if he didn't. I explain the clichéd but functional term to him as we drive up the winding road from his house towards mountain-sheltered D'Arcy. Polite silence from the passenger seat as he considers and then rejects my term.

"It's not one I'd use," he says politely. "I'd just call it like-minded people."

"But you knew I'd call, didn't you?"

"Yeah, when the time was right."

The time is right – and a bit fragile – and he knows it. The response is unfailingly kind and gentle, as I guessed it would be.

"So," he says, "the situation didn't work out the way you expected. How do you feel about that?"

Feel. The word drops my defenses, eliminates small talk. Hands tight on the wheel, eyes steady on the curving highway, I answer. "Not good. As though I've been in a car accident."

Honestly didn't think I would speak about this. Thought I could stay quiet, numb or perhaps joke about the "many-splendored" thing called romance. Such a relief to know that subterfuge and deflection are not necessary. It's been a tough week; from what I can sense, this guy's had a few of those in his time, too.

Halfway to D'Arcy, but hungry now, ready for lunch. We stop beside a narrow, fast-flowing river to eat our picnic. In the present moment again, our psyches lightened by the sharing of food and stories of ocean, travel and family.

Much talk of family.

The references to his children are frequent and affectionate. Adults now, the daughter and son have created lives their father is comfortable watching unfold, has respect for. My friend goes beyond a simple listing of work and life choices and underscores their ability to commit – to goals, ideals and people. I watch the shadings in his eyes and realize he is committed, too; a marriage dissolved, but a family sphere only redefined, strengthened.

Onto the lake. Day to evening, evening to darkness. In Pemberton, another meal enjoyed. Bounty before us, we speak of other hungers, the ones that food and drink do not relieve.

"Do you believe in God?" At thirty-five, I can say the word easily, feel no embarrassment at my reliance on prayer.

"No." His tone is matter-of-fact, unequivocal.

"But what do you do, when the tidal waves come along?"

"Write. Think it out. Move on."

We exchange an amused look, mutual incomprehension a point of interest, not conflict. Many paths to the shores of serenity. What counts is the arrival.

Tired now, and many miles to go before I sleep. Perhaps he wouldn't mind …

"Do you think I could …?"

"I have a fold-out couch in the living room."

"Would it be okay, if …?"

"The dog can sleep with you."

In the morning I awake early. Before our first cup of coffee I am already thinking about story deadlines and how good it will feel to sit in front of my computer, focused and intent. I thank my friend for his hospitality and open the door to my car for the dog to jump in the back seat.

"Stay in touch," I say.

He smiles, "I will."

The waters of Howe Sound are brilliant under the full sun. The car seems to drive itself as my mind busily turns over the diverse topics of conversation my friend and I covered during my visit: books, writing, work, self-care and meeting the challenge of emotional upheavals. Our coping mechanisms, as it turned out, were dissimilar: one called on reason, the other on spirit.

No matter. We're both prepared to take icy dives and rise up with challenge in our eyes.

# 5

## LONG-DISTANCE FRIENDSHIP

*MAY 1996, VANCOUVER, BRITISH COLUMBIA*

It's 7:00 p.m. – he's phoned the last two nights at this time, it might be Don. I pick up the phone, skip the greeting and take a chance it's him. "You can't have the essays yet!" I laugh. "I just mailed them today!" *Please, let it be him, I love talking to him so much.*

"No," says Don, "I just wanted to know how your interview with the UFAWU guy went today. You said you were a bit nervous about it."

Dennis Brown, at the United Fishermen and Allied Workers Union – oh yes, I was right to be a little on edge about that. Hard to get a word in edgewise with that man, not to mention that he answers, at length, every question you haven't asked him. At least he's gender-blind, which doesn't happen often in the commercial or sport fishing worlds. Union-brother and all that. So yeah, it went all right in the end and I got what I needed to meet my deadline for *Fishermen's News* in Seattle, Washington, this coming Friday. The pay's lousy but I love being their monthly Canadian correspondent. Usually get a nice layout too.

I tell Don all this and he tells me his writerly news. We are only just starting to talk more about personal matters.

"How are you feeling these days?" I ask.

Sometimes he can talk about this, sometimes not. Sometimes he sounds so weary and heartsick I have to ask him, gently, to speak up, because his voice drops below discernible pitch. And sometimes, even often, his voice is lit by love and longing. That's when he's telling me Lulu stories.

"The love doesn't go anywhere, does it?" I say. "Just because she's gone doesn't mean the love is any less intense – it's probably more intense. But it's as though the love has no home anymore. You're holding onto it, it's yours by right, and yet you don't know what to do with it anymore, where to put it. You've got the sun, but no sky to put it in." Death or a breakup, I think, you never know what to do with the leftover love.

He begins to respond, then his voice breaks. He is weeping. The sound goes straight to my own tattered heart. The tawdry ending to my latest romantic mistake is only one month old. The man seemed a good bet – near my age, fun to hike, fish and adventure with – and none of it meant anything when we became lovers. That itself was a chilly endeavour, followed by worse. I've had trouble knowing when to cut my losses, with both friends and sweethearts, preferring to believe the best of people. I've also been known to engage in "magical" or false thinking, the sort that is harmful, as it keeps cold but true reality at arm's length. This was surely true in this case.

I envy Don his pure, guiltless heartbreak. I've never lost a sweetheart to an implacable Fate. Mostly the reasons are more complicated and convoluted – though there's certainly been stubborn naivety and poor judgment on my part. Or indifference, now and again, on someone's part. But I don't know – *burned to death or drowned* – does one sort of loss really hurt more than another? I know self-forgiveness has to figure in here somewhere, I just have trouble finding it some days.

"We should say good night for now," I suggest to Don. He had cried only briefly, then resolutely talked of other more neutral subjects. I like his resiliency, the calm he's able to find after his storms. It is I who feels anything but resilient this evening. Sometimes my own heartache is all I can manage. "Maybe we can talk later in the week?"

I wonder how self-forgiveness would feel – not just imaginings or glimpses of it, but living it, every day?

# 6

## The Forming Years

### January 11, 2011, Halifax, Nova Scotia

My life is so civilized and peaceful there are days I could weep with gratitude. The life I have created with my husband over the past fifteen years allows me to write freelance articles and personal letters, teach memoir writing, read, cook the meals we like to eat, play a little music now and then, sail and travel within Canada and internationally, spend time with family and friends, far-flung and nearby. We loved our dog Leo, who we often simply called The Whippet, and we love our new little companion, MacTavish the Shetland sheepdog, or Sheltie. Leo was a gentleman, never cross or argumentative. MacTavish, or Tavish, as we usually call him, is a stronger cup of tea. This matters not one iota. I call him the "bad biker boyfriend" because we love him extravagantly and unstoppably, bossy traits, barking and all. There is no way we have discovered to be immune to his extreme beauty and shocking intelligence. Despite his natural reserve, poor creature, we maul him constantly. We are rewarded with brief but intense shows of affection. MacTavish has only been in our lives for five years. We are a work in progress, we three.

My life is also charmed, rich in blessings. I love and I am loved. I enjoy and I am enjoyed. I am safe from all psychic harms or physical discomforts. Don thinks I am the funniest person he's ever met; this is ridiculously important to me. On March 14, 2011, we will celebrate our thirteenth wedding anniversary. I can still miss him when he is in the next room. We exchanged over eight hundred e-mails before we shared our first kiss, along with countless phone calls and regular mail communications. We still e-mail one another every day of our lives.

Four years into our life in the city, other precious bits are falling into place as well. To my intense joy, I am on the verge of having horses in my life again on a regular basis. I knew Halifax would come through for me! Hammonds Plains Road – a.k.a., suburban horse land. Not as ritzy or diverse as Southlands – no hunt clubs or polo fields, no hacking trails along a river and through the deep woods to long beaches – but horse land for sure, complete with private barns for family horse owners, schooling barns that offer boarding facilities, lessons, monthly leases and small horse shows, and right in this same neighbourhood, a top-notch tack store run by an astute businesswoman.

The world of horses keeps changing and changing – methods, philosophies, tack, clothing, boots, even the horses themselves, various breeds coming in and out of style and general availability – and I have changed too. I am a long way from fit, and a longer way from the 104 pounds I weighed when I met Don. Neither reality aids riding, but I am working to change both, as best I can. All in good time. I am now two lessons to the better of being unfit. After ten mostly horseless years in Cape Breton, the time is *now* to get my riding seat back.

Luck has guided me to a great schooling barn and the perfect instructor for my circumstances. She's in her forties, I think, and I'm fifty-two, but our riding backgrounds are similar. I understand her riding experiences and motivations and she understands mine; I also see a bit of my mum in her, in her devotion to a nine-year-old daughter who lives only to ride, only to breathe in all the assertive smells of a barn. Unlike my mother, who only rode as a child and teenager, my instructor still rides and competes.

My impossibly generous and loving mother ... she kept waiting for me to outgrow my need and love for horses – and she never seemed to understand what it took to go back to the barn after we lost Karin. Six months later, I finally said goodbye to handsome, talented Coqeyn, the horse of any young girl's dreams. With the sale, I gave away all our expensive German-made tack – it was Coqeyn's, he deserved it – pressed my cheek to the warm soft spot between his nostrils and fled the barn, heart-scalded and instantly amnesiac. Karin, Karin – where had you *gone*? How could I *do* this alone? I wasn't good enough, smart enough. Coqeyn, forgive me, I was used to loving you both together. I had to step away, heal, come back when the shadows in barns came and went with the seasons, not with my memories.

Maybe our mother understood all these things and thought it was further folly. I felt like a child, shamed and tentative when she expressed her disapproval of my reconnection to the horse world in my twenties. When I kept on riding into my thirties, she was nonplussed.

"Going to the barn!" I'd crow, breeches tight, field boots shined and long hair in a swinging pony tail. The hours and lessons piled up; I was a better rider by far than I had been as a teenager. I imagined a healthy, new Karin cheering me on, knew she'd be proud. Mum would purse her lips and shake her head. I could hear the silent question clear as a symphony: *Nothing better to do?* and her own answer: *You're too old for this.*

As with most of the family, I struggled so hard with depression – she did too, it's in the journals she left behind, from teenage years on – and knew in my bones that horses kept me moving, kept me sane. I didn't really want to say that to my mother – the keeping sane part. She'd had enough of craziness during the interminable Karin years. Before that it was the dramatic and showy departure of her husband that made her a stick figure in her clothes and too poor to buy ones that fit. Every cent she earned went to looking after her four children and paying the mortgage on the big beautiful house on

Vancouver's southwest side. That she was first able to do this driving a cab at night – "I have too much education," she explained. "No one wants to hire me as a clerk or a secretary – I won't stay, they think" – was a miracle, duly aided by taking on a second mortgage.

In time she would take a "fifth-year-Ed" degree to add onto her honours philosophy and English B.A. from the University of Toronto. Next to her adventurous, travel-filled time in the Air Force ("Sgt. Atkinson"), her twenty-odd years of teaching high school were among the happiest of her life.

But not those early years. Along with the shrunken body came a depression and despair so heavy it tore at all our hearts to witness. Never a word of complaint, just the silent screaming rage we all knew vibrated within her, and the gut-twisting feeling of inadequacy in all of us children that we Couldn't Make It Right.

How could we? We were eight, ten, thirteen and fifteen when Richard Beaufort Simmins began his adulterous affair with a co-worker. "Vancouver Art Gallery Director Fired; Leaves Wife and Four Children for Adulterous Affair" – maybe the newspaper headlines didn't announce exactly that, but all the chattering, bourgeois families around us did. We Five, Mum and her four children, not my father or *married* lover, were looked upon as social lepers. We all lost friends when it happened, and my mother always maintained that she was "dropped like a hot potato" by all their associates at the gallery and even most of their personal and artist friends.

Divorce in the late 1960s was a terrible, morally degenerate disease That Was Not Done By Decent Families. "Oh," said a dear friend of mine from early school years, "my parents would *never* get divorced." To her and her family's credit, they remained loyal to us. To my credit, I did not remind her of her statement when her parents did indeed divorce, not so many years later. But we were among the first "broken" families.

An alcoholic at that time, Dad always claimed that his new love "saved his life." This she did, he said, by allowing him to love himself for the first time in his life. I don't know how she did that, exactly, but I do know, we all did, that she refused to be with him until he quit drinking. His sobriety came after a nervous breakdown, as they termed a collapse in those days, and with the lifelong aid of Alcoholics Anonymous.

Dad and his sweetheart had a passionate and tumultuous relationship for fourteen years. She never divorced or even "left" her husband and three teenage children, though she and Dad lived together on and off, in different cities, during this time. Dad asked her numerous times to marry him. She refused every time. At the cusp of the 1980s he decided to ask one more time, yet again telling her how important it was to him to marry "the love of his life." She refused. He left her, without a backward glance. Within weeks, maybe months, she became ill with stomach cancer. He refused to even visit her in the hospital and she died, I presume, with her family around her. "She adored me," said Dad, shrugging his shoulders, "but loved her husband and family, too." She had also been raised poor, and had a terror of being poor again, he explained. Who knew how she'd come out of a divorce, in terms of finances. Divorce, fourteen ultimate and tattered years later, Was Not Done In Her Family.

Dad knew I and everyone in his family hated his girlfriend for her role in splitting up our family. Years later, when I met the girlfriend's charming and artistic daughter (I never met the two sons), I became painfully aware of the other side of the affair's equation: my father, too, had devastated a family, entered their midst like an atomic bomb. All of us children had trouble trusting Dad again. What helped, immeasurably, were the rules by which our father now lived his life, à la Alcoholics Anonymous. He used these wisdoms to heal many of the fractured relationships in his life and to guide his interactions with his adult children. We spoke of the past, therefore, only briefly and lived forgiveness as best we could. I knew how he had lacerated himself for his past decisions and I watched in wonder as he moved past self-loathing to a place of self-acceptance and peace. "I am a beautiful, ugly man," he'd say, shrugging again. "I do the best I can."

I think he was a lucky man, too. None of us ever stopped loving him – Barbara Atkinson Simmins and we children from that union – though our hearts were confused and wary for many years.

Exit Dad's girlfriend, enter Karin Weiss. When blonde-haired, blue-eyed, thirty-three-year-old Karin Weiss entered the Ottawa bookstore Dad owned late in 1980, she was a woman "on a mission," as we used to say when I was a teenager. She wanted to be married and she wanted to have children. Karin thought a man like Dad, who she found attractive, intelligent and excellent, amusing company, might be just the sort of man with whom she'd choose to share a life and start a family.

*Karin?* we three adult children asked in horrified wonder. Is her name truly *Karin? Children*, we repeated stonily. You want more *children?* At age fifty-five?

Apparently.

It was a long story, of course – there was a marriage and children and another fourteen-year relationship. But calm, welcoming Karin enjoyed the company of her husband's grown-up children and did everything in her power to make sure we had alone-time with Dad and together-time with them both and our new young sisters. Karin had nothing to do with painful pasts and everything to do with sunny presents. She still does.

So much to explain to Don, in the beginning. Which was why it seemed easier to *show* him some of the stories about my parents, with my essays, than to tell him.

## Of Dad And Dandelions
### Ottawa, Ontario, 1996

I lie face down in a yard of long grass and dandelions. The sun is warm on my back and grass blades tickle my nose. Despite the heat, the ground is slightly damp; I smell the earth beneath me and wonder briefly if it is nearly as rich as the delta lands where I live, thousands of miles from this place. I feel relaxed; I could almost fall asleep this way. Just need to stretch out that left arm a little bit –

"Very still," comes the request from three metres above on the veranda. And then, several shutter-clicks later, "OK, think I got it." I shrug and shake to my feet, bits of grass stuck to my hands, my jeans spotted with circles of yellow from the press of the flowers. A quick climb over the neighbour's fence and I am back, sitting at the picnic table outside my father's house.

"You'll like that one," says my photographer father, his camera in constant, creative use in the past few years. "Trust me."

I do trust him. Of the three rolls of film developed in the past week, there were only a few photos I didn't much like. Not bad, technically speaking; they simply showed thirty-seven-year-old me looking more sombre than usual. "No teeth" shots, Dad calls them. The dandelion pose was fun. If it works out, it will match the dominant tone of my visit thus far.

"More coffee?"

He shakes his head; we've had two already and it's almost time to start supper, a stir-fry tonight. We will work side by side in the kitchen, washing and slicing vegetables purchased at the farmer's market earlier this afternoon. Red bell peppers, snow peas, carrots, broccoli, celery – a mix of colour as vibrant as the green and gold in the yard next to us.

It's been two years since we've seen each other. Dad has already informed me that I haven't aged, and I am trying to figure out why he looks younger than he did the last time I came to Ottawa. Considering the upheavals in both our lives in the past year, we should both be looking decidedly worse for wear.

Dad's not the only one taking photos. I am busy recording mental images of a family who in a month – when his wife, my stepmother, leaves to set up a home on her own – will no longer be together. The atmosphere in the house is curiously calm, even affectionate; I sense no bitterness, hear no words of anger or recrimination. Still, change is coming and I am uneasy, especially for my two half-sisters, Jessica, thirteen, and Fiona, nine.

I remember two things about being nine: it was the year my math phobia began and the time when I finally accepted my father's permanent absence from the family home. It had been a year since he'd left, but the lack of a formal parting had confused me: father present, father gone – really gone. After a while he came back for a visit, but that was equally confusing: Christmas celebrations awkward and surreal; the silent clamour of unmet needs and desires; the glowering, judgemental eyes of my older siblings. In the end I saw his departure as a void, colourless and deep.

Unlike people, voids cannot be hurt. Resentment and anger do not affect them. Hate the void, love the father: child's logic, off-centre and comforting. It served me well for some years, but it never took away the dread of goodbyes.

"We're in good shape, aren't we?"

His question pulls me back to a late afternoon of lilac-scented breeze and weakening sun. I look across the table to his age-creased, smiling face. His observation is truthful, not voiced in false bravado. He is in good shape – body, mind and spirit – and so am I.

We have talked about the challenges that lie ahead. In the past week, I have scrutinized Jessica's and Fiona's faces as closely as I now do our father's. I have seen ripples of sadness but, overall, an understanding that they are loved. They know, from their parents' actions and words, that these feelings will not change. What will change is that they will have two homes, each headed by a parent who will provide care and attention. A void of unity, but not of any one individual. As for their grown-up siblings, Zoë, Geoffrey and me, the future will prove our commitment to the girls.

We rise from the table to begin supper chores. I think, but do not say, how much I like sharing these activities with him: enjoyment of the mundane, taken too early from the years we lived together. Tidy the house, set the table, light the candles. Life-sustaining trivia, my older sister calls it. Dad and I move smoothly around the kitchen. Another photo, tucked into the mind's album.

After supper, a reversal of the initial process: table cleared, dishes stacked and washed, kitchen tidied. The candles on the dining room table, however, remain lit. Time for Yahtzee. Dad and I have played this dice game for as long as I can remember. A generally mindless diversion, it serves, in our case, a time-honoured purpose. As soon as the dice start rattling in the shaker cup, conversation kicks into high gear. The exchanges have a peculiar, long-established pattern, beginning in the far past and then settling into the present. Decades-old relationships are invariably the starting point. We speak of people of whom we have a shared picture. In recent years, there hasn't often been the opportunity to meet, face to face, new players on the stage. But sooner or later our talk comes around to the present.

"What about the fellow … ?" His question straggles off as he considers whether to stick with a high roll or try once more for a higher one. Triumphant, he rolls a six, asks again about a man he's never met and now never will meet. The discussion is brief: over, gone and mostly done with. It's the "mostly" part that Dad is concerned about. I surprise myself by keeping my own counsel on the subject. Surprised, because my father is a direct man who elicits direct answers, and I am too often accommodating when I want to stand firm. I am not ready to share particulars at this time; I will when I have a better sense of resolution. I roll a Yahtzee – five identical dice – and we call it a night.

The next morning I awake to the hum of a motor. The neighbour's yard has become a short-cropped, flower-free lawn. Unlike yesterday, when hundreds of small, glowing suns caught the eye, the yard is now quite ordinary. I point; Dad turns with the gesture and looks back at me with a smile. Catch the moment, swim toward the colour. Could be gone sooner than you think.

At the airport I sip root beer from a plastic cup. Ten minutes before my flight is called, I am detached enough to be partway home already. Will there be one paycheque or two waiting for me? And what about the dog, will he sulk for a day, or will a few hugs and biscuits claim his heart again?

When my flight is called the familiar tension begins. I know it is no longer necessary to feel this fear. If only he could reverse the order of our greetings: welcome me with goodbyes, leave me with hellos. Above all, assure me there will be a next time. I want to believe this in my bones.

His arms are tight around me and words that have taken over twenty-five years to believe are offered to the air: "We'll see each other again." His tone is certain, with a top note of surprise as though he, too, believes this for the first time. A wash of colour fills the void. This is no lie offered for a child's comfort; it is truth, bright as the gold of a dandelion. I will see my father again. Eyes tender, hearts easy, we part with hellos.

## WRITING THE DISTANCES AWAY
### VANCOUVER, BRITISH COLUMBIA, 1992

A letter arrives from my father this morning. It has travelled from Ottawa to Richmond in a square white envelope, addressed in a script fine enough to adorn a medieval scroll. I tuck the letter in my shirt pocket, pour myself a cup of coffee and return to my workroom, where the computer hums and an autumn sun casts long shadows onto my desk.

I will open the letter in an hour or so, when I have folded down all the corners of my impatience: letters are to be savoured, before and after the contents are known.

Most people would rather have a root canal performed than write a letter. I've never understood why. For my family, letter writing is a need and a pleasure; during the year, hundreds of letters will cross between Ottawa, Calgary, Ladner, Richmond and York, England. I will receive over one hundred from my father alone. The post office loves the Simmins family.

It is not only the process of writing and sharing our lives that we enjoy, it is also the selection of materials and pens. Some of us choose thick bond paper and fountain pens; others choose gold-flecked rice paper and fine-tipped ball points. Themes and interests within each of our lives are reflected in stationery patterns and cards: horses, blue herons, Japanese art, fish boats, pressed flowers, architecture, gardens. Envelopes are multi-hued, and often closed with red sealing wax and gold-inked stamps. One page short or ten pages long, the letters are read and carefully collected in boxes, desks and journals.

"But so many! What do you write about?" asked a Vancouver friend of mine not long ago. "It would get to the point where you'd have to discuss the grocery list."

As a matter of fact, we do discuss food: "Went to the Byward Market this afternoon. Bought a basket of ripe field tomatoes – perfect for frying with a bit of sugar – and an armload of vegetables, most of them still sprinkled with the black earth of the Ottawa Valley ..." "The wharf at Steveston was crazy-busy today. Couldn't resist the prawns, piled high in tubs of ice. Took two pounds. I'll cook them in butter, add a squeeze of lime and serve with curried rice and papaya ..." "Nothing like Alberta beef. Joan and I are expecting forty guests for dinner tonight. We'll barbecue a roast, loaded with fresh-ground pepper and slivers of garlic ..." "I didn't plant as big a garden as usual this year, but there's still plenty of vegetables to take us through the fall. The carrots are small and sweet, just the way Jocelyn loves them ..."

We discuss other types of nourishment as well: books, movies, theatre, our work – and the people with whom we share a home and a daily existence. If we didn't detail these thoughts, I would not know, for example, that my one-month-old nephew prefers to look up at the world, bold and inquiring; "... he is firmly determined not to be put on his stomach, and will instantly flip over on his back, whenever we move him." Nor would my brother know, for a heart-on-paper-certainty, that his child is welcomed and loved by all his family months before they will hold the baby in their arms. Not so long from now, the letters will begin to arrive addressed to my nephew. This nurturing word-flow is part of his heritage.

Letters provide a continuity in our long-distance relationships that phone calls and infrequent visits cannot match. It is the process of living that is most important – instead of simply being told something has occurred, we are privy to the anticipation and after-effects of significant events. Triumphs are recognized with exclamation marks and underlined phrases; sorrows are described in untidy, unpunctuated paragraphs. We read, absorb and respond.

As with conversations, the words not spoken in letters are as revealing as the ones that are. We note the absence of certain names and adjectives and look beneath the words for the more subtle clues to mood and outlook. We do not question the level of intimacy offered, nor do we draw back when support is requested. With each letter mailed, we offer one-on-one attention and inclusion.

And there's the key: inclusion. Wherever we go or whatever we are doing, we try to step outside our own perspective and draw in the person we are thinking of that day. If something tastes superb, feels right or sounds exquisite – I take a pen and share the moment; it increases my enjoyment double-fold.

Living so far apart, we could easily lose the rhythm of our laughter and affection, but we resist this loss, with every postcard and each sheet of paper that passes through our hands.

Letters are songs. Our voices rise clear and steady over the miles.

## THE HOUSE WITH MANY DOORS
### — FOR MUM —
#### HALIFAX, NOVA SCOTIA, 2013

Vancouver, 1968

People are always leaving. There are many doors inside our house and three doors leading out of our house. People move from room to room, upstairs and down, then to the basement rooms, slamming doors behind them. There are bells tied to the curtain rod on the back door. The bells jangle when the door is slammed shut. The front door is heavy. My brother uses it the most. My mum and sisters don't slam that one. They prefer the lighter doors. You don't have to be angry to slam a door. You might just want to be heard for some reason. Everyone in the house slams doors. Or just shuts them hard. It's how we talk right now.

I step through one of the five doorways leading into the kitchen. The room is empty and cold. I could go back upstairs, get a sweater. But I don't want to wake Mum. Sometimes she has a mid-morning nap on Saturdays. Once she was sleeping so hard I couldn't even shake her awake. That scared me. No more Valium, she says now. Now she wakes easily again. I stood in the doorway of her room before I came back downstairs. Face to the wall, she had turned over, said, "Hello, little love," then rolled back to the wall again. She looks funny in that small bed in my brother's old room.

Which reminds me. I slip through two doors into my parents' old bed-room. The double bed is made up tidily and there are books in the shelf of the headboard. The books are boring. I've checked them many times. But there are things on the bureau that interest me. 711 Eau de Parfum. A paisley ascot. One cufflink. Parent stuff. Beyond these, a bottle I can just reach.

Aqua Velva aftershave. The turquoise liquid makes the centre of me go soft with colour-happiness. Could be mermaid water. The bottle is almost full. He will return for it. And for us, of course.

Karin, my red-haired sister, five years older than me, scorns me for this idea. "You really think he's coming back, don't you?" she asked last week, when she caught me smelling the aftershave. She shook her head: "Stupid." She melted away.

My red-haired sister can appear out of nowhere; she doesn't even need doors. She has a hunger to hurt, like a nasty cat with sharp claws. She scratches Mum, mostly. Mum pretends it doesn't hurt. We all look away, because it hurts everyone, but we don't know what to do. Fourteen years old and she frightens all of us. That's the reason the mermaid water helps. Just for a moment of softness inside. I think my red-haired sister misses Dad, even though she says she hates him. It feels like she hates all of us.

She is staying at a friend's house this weekend. I am glad.

. Zoë, my blonde-haired sister, seven years older than me, isn't here very much these days. Dad left last year, when the snowdrops came up in the garden. My blonde-haired sister's face is like a whole garden of flowers since she met her boyfriend, also last year. But she is furious at Dad, too.

I think I'll watch some TV. "Idiot box," my parents call it. But Mum enjoys it more than Dad ever did. On Friday nights we all watch TV together. We have "Friday night treats," a phrase Mum made up. TGIF, she says on a Friday night – thank God it's Friday. We pass around bowls of jujubes and Bridge Mixture and pieces of Burnt Almond chocolate bars. We aren't allowed Coke during the week, but we drink it on Friday night. Everyone seems lighter, happier on a Friday night.

I look up from *Captain Kangaroo* to see my mother.

"Hungry?" she asks.

I had Tang and toast, and tell her this. I even remembered to put the glass and plate in the sink, and didn't leave it here on the table in front of me in the family room. She hates it when we eat in here, and make a mess. My brother is twelve and I am nine; we don't do much housework. Mum used to do it throughout the day, along with the ironing, grocery shopping and meal making. Now she drives a cab and can't keep up with the housework or the gardening. This distresses her. She loves order and tidiness.

"We had maids growing up," she says sometimes. My sisters, brother and I find it hard to picture this. Maids are for rich people, not for people with second mortgages and cars that need repair.

We had a home in London, Ontario, and a cottage on the lake, in Bayfield, she explains, eyes distant with happy memories. Why, I didn't even know how to cook, she'd tell us with pride, until after the Air Force, when I went to university. Her roommates teased her into the kitchen, she said.

My father's new girlfriend – "Daddy's *whore*," says my red-haired sister – is a very good cook, our father tells us. This knowledge hurts me.

It is too quiet in the kitchen. I look over my shoulder from my spot on the couch. Mum is standing in the centre of the room. Her shoulders are rising up and down. It looks like she is laughing.

Sadness and anger. With Mum, it's hard to pry those two feelings apart. Sometimes I think she's just sad and then I see the shimmer of rage in her eyes. Mostly I see fatigue. I feel bad. Our lives feel so heavy sometimes. I can't find the right things to do, to make Mum feel better.

I stand in the doorway. Everything is still around us, except for a boiling kettle on the stove. Mum hasn't had her tea yet. This hurts me too. Too much sadness, even before her first cup of sugared, black tea. Of the five purple doors, four are closed. All that dark colour set against white. Somehow it seems like the room is pushing in. It's hard to breathe in this cold place.

"I am going to pack us a bag," she says. "We are going away."

Now I really can't breathe. My brother. He's downstairs sleeping. If he wakes up and we are gone, maybe he'll go, too. He isn't mean like my red-haired sister and he's here most of the time. We laugh together, listen to records. He's teaching me how to play poker. I can't lose him, too.

"I'll write a note for your brother. He'll be fine for a day."

I open my mouth and a spiral of distress comes out. A cat, her tail stepped on.

"Stop it. It's only today and part of tomorrow." She is moving briskly now, talking to herself. "Write a note, put it by his place at the table; don't forget a book, need a book, and sweaters, too ..."

Vancouver is a pearl today. From a cold kitchen we step out to a mild, blossom-scented world. The clouds are gold-rimmed and tumbling on a north-west wind, the sky behind a light-shot blue. The navy blue ocean has curled white tips on it, like the boiled icing you put on an angel food cake. We drive alongside English Bay. Saturday morning and the downtown streets are busy. Sailboats skim by the Planetarium. Farther out in the harbour there are orange-bottomed freighters. Yellow and red popcorn stands are set one block apart all along Pacific Avenue. My breakfast has worn off and the scent of buttery popped corn makes my stomach grumble. I wonder when we'll stop, where we are going to spend the night.

The Cove Motel is on Denman Street. The beach is two minutes away. Our room has two beds, a sitting room and a kitchenette. Mum has brought food from home. For lunch we have soda crackers, cheddar cheese, and fruit and sultana cookies. Mum has her tea, I have a Coke. It's not Friday. But I have a Coke. It's warm but good. The room is warm, too. The table where we eat lunch is set beneath two big windows. We watch the lacy curtains pull back and forth with the wind from the open window. We are silent, watching the material breathe so easily. In time, our own breaths match the rhythm.

We go to the beach. The harbour has even more sailboats in it now. We walk at the ocean's edge and squeal when the waves touch the toes of our shoes. Turning, we stop at a popcorn vendor's and buy a bag of popcorn. The paper bag is slick with butter, the popcorn, spilling over the top, is hot and delicious.

Back at our room we take off our wet shoes and socks. Mum is pleased that she remembered our slippers. We change into cozy clothes and book-end the couch, our stories in hand. We read in silence.

I could tell her. I could tell her that Dad is coming back. That she won't have to drive a taxi anymore, and we won't have to have another family share the house this autumn, so Mum can train to be a teacher. I can't make my blonde-haired sister come home more often, and none of us are safe from my red-haired sister's claws. My brother likes to laugh, but mostly, he's as angry and sad as Mum. He really misses Dad. I guess I can't fix that, either. I don't even know when, exactly, Dad is coming back. All the same, I should tell her: *We're going to be all right, Mum.*

I start to speak and then look up at my mother's intent reading face. Not just intent but soft. I haven't seen peace on my mother's face in many months.

She looks up, finds my studying eyes, smiles.

"I am going to teach you a game. It's called honeymoon bridge."

Out come the cards and scorepad. I am not good at the game but I like it. It's a grown-up game, like poker, but it's also our game, Mum's and mine. *Trump. Singleton. Bluffing. Suits. Void.* All these fun new words and ideas. I like to watch her hands when she shuffles and deals the cards. Her movements are tidy. Calm, somehow, too.

We play until dark, eat a peanut butter and banana sandwich, and prepare to sleep in separate beds. I thought we'd share a bed.

"I love you," she says, smiling, "but you kick and thrash in your sleep."

The next morning she is awake before I am and rises quickly. Yesterday is far away. Today is already heavy on her shoulders. She makes tea, packs away the cards and our belongings.

"Your brother," she says – the thin sound of her voice scares me – "I must phone him." She calls my brother. He was worried, Mum tells me, hanging up the receiver. He wants us to come home. We hurry around the room, straightening bedcovers and washing and drying our dishes. When we leave, there is nothing to say we were ever in the room.

*What in the name of God was I thinking,* I hear her mutter.

I am glad we're going home. I need to hear a few slamming doors. People do leave our house, but they come back home, too. My blonde-haired sister will be home today, and we'll all have supper together; sometimes she and I sing "Frère Jacques" in rounds when we dry the supper dishes. My red-haired sister still won't be back until tomorrow. My brother won't be sad or mad today, he'll be glad we are back.

Sometimes I think that Dad may not come back. He doesn't really like that cravat on the bureau, and I guess he can buy more aftershave. *Replaceable.* Things. People. I hadn't thought of that before. My stomach returns to its usual twisted place. Then I look at Mum. Even worried, her face isn't as tight as it was yesterday. She touches my cheek.

"We'll be all right, little love," she says. We drive to the house with many doors. We enter through the back door and bring the sound of bells with us.

# 7

## *Be Careful What You Ask For*

### June 1996, Vancouver, British Columbia

Dear God: Please send me someone to love. *Be careful what you ask for, lest the gods should* –

I can't do this. I just can't. I didn't understand that he *liked* me – not until the last few weeks, when he's made that focus clear. Don wants to be my lover – and that's not where I saw this relationship going. I mean, give me a break – his oldest "child," a son who lives in Ottawa, is two years younger than I am. Twenty-two years is just too much of an age gap. I don't want an affair. I want a long-term, loving relationship. Marriage. With someone close to my age.

On the other hand, there was twenty-five years between my father and my stepmother, Karin Weiss. Yes, they've separated now – there aren't any guarantees in life – but I saw a lot of joy in those various Ottawa households over the years. It is Dad who says, whenever a whiff of criticism comes near Karin, "Fourteen years of peace, that's what Karin gave me, fourteen years of peace." It doesn't matter how we adult children view the matter – nor should it. But loyalty to Dad aside, even we can see the most obvious truth. Dad adores Karin, she loved him with all her heart for many years, and the marriage produced two beautiful daughters, Jessica and Fiona. Their breakup is hard to watch and learn about, but it's one of the more civil and kind ones I've seen.

Now that I think about it, that last relationship of mine was hideously hurtful – and that man was the "perfect" age for me, two and a half years older, same age as my wonderful brother, who he never did get to meet. So there goes the age compatibility theory, right out the door –

No, this is crazy. Don has five children – three biological children and two adopted – and no interest in having any more. And I don't want to live anywhere but Vancouver! I love my life here, if not my love life. I can't compromise on everything, can I?

I can't believe I am even thinking these things. I am embarrassed. Who the hell says Silver Donald Cameron would ever want to marry me? Where the hell did that conceited thought come from?

*Why does he have to be so wonderful to talk to?*

I told Don about those early conversations with Dad, how I hovered on the edge of freelancing for so long. I was reluctant, even post-B.A., to bid adieu to the steady and abundant cash of my waitressing jobs. These were also post-commercial fishing years, I explained, post-breakup with the fisherman I spent nearly a decade with and jilted one month before we were to be married.

*Jilted? A month before you married?* That must have been terribly hard on everyone, said Don.

Can we talk about that another time? I asked him. My mind had gone to the whitest shade of blank. All I can hear is the music from that awful time in my life: John Lee Hooker, Stevie Ray Vaughan and Margo Timmins from Cowboy Junkies, singing "Misguided Angel."

I'm sorry – what was I –

Your dad, prompted Don. You were talking about your dad and how you finally started freelancing.

Right, yes, thanks. Ummm, well – my dad was a former freelance arts journalist himself. He was so sure I could be a freelancer. Much surer than I was. I'd ask him, Dad, what would I write about?

And he'd ask, What do you know about, what do you love? Then I knew – it hit me like a bolt out of the literal blue: *Fish, I know a lot about fish.*

I told Don all this and he just kept asking more questions – because the journalist in him knew it wasn't the whole story. Sure, I knew about fish from the years of working as a deckhand and yes, and I revered the five wild salmon species the way only a West Coaster can, salmon being a religion in the Pacific Northwest and Alaska. I loved the whole vast ocean world and all its creatures from Orcas and Dall's porpoises to orange and purple sea stars, bull kelp and the tiniest krill. He understood all of that and how the fisheries could be an obvious choice for me to start freelancing about.

There's something else here, though, he said. I can hear it in your voice.

*Then I won't speak,* I thought. I would count, silently. It's what I do when I get scared. (– *one, two, three, four* –)

Hello? said Don. Marjorie, are you still there?

(– *five, six, seven* –) The essays (– *eight, nine, ten* –) sometimes I write them for my fisherman. I write them (– *eleven, twelve, thirteen* –) hoping he'll see them.

So now he knows that many of the essays or articles are intended for my fisherman's eyes, understands the coded language of love and regret in many of the pieces. Sometimes I'd write "service articles" so my fisherman could have useful marine information, I explained. Sometimes I'd write humour pieces and hope he found them funny. God, I missed laughing with him. Sometimes I'd see something that made me think of him so sharply, the longing stayed for hours, like the hot ache of a jellyfish's sting. So I'd write about it, to ease the feelings.

I was in it this far, so I carried on: Almost all of my personal essays are coded for someone, I said, whether or not they're still in my life. For those who aren't, it's a way of saying the things you didn't have the opportunity or guts to say to them when you were together. Like a second chance to get it right, even if they never read the essay – which of course I would never know anyway. But I like to imagine they do read the essays and maybe feel a bit of regret and longing themselves. Regardless, I've said what I needed to say, to move on with my life, inch by inch.

Don knows *all* this now – and he still likes me, doesn't think I am daft. In fact, as I said a moment ago, he thinks I am ... *quite all right*, really.

*(– one, two, three, four –)*

"When I saw you walking along Broadway to the café, that first time we met," he said, the last time we spoke, "I couldn't believe my eyes. I'd been told that *Trek Magazine* was sending one of its best writers to interview me, that she was also a commercial fisheries reporter. I figured you'd be a Viking lady, four axe handles across the backside and biceps bulging. And there you were, a pretty blonde woman in a short skirt and high heels. And you know how much fun we had talking that day." He started laughing, obviously having fun on this day, too. "I told my wife, when I got home to Cape Breton from the trip, 'I will never be unfaithful to you, but if I were going to be, it might have been last weekend in Vancouver.'"

Flattered but appalled, I asked, What did Lulu say?

"Oh, she laughed," he said. "She thought it was very funny."

Are you sure? I asked. Seems an unusual response. One could even say evolved. *Quite beyond my cavewoman ways,* I thought to myself.

"Yes," chuckled Don. "She was evolved in that way – not jealous or possessive. But she also knew she had nothing to worry about, ever. I was a very happy man."

His voice stayed steady throughout this conversation. I even heard him smiling. Sometimes happy memories are just – happy. And sometimes the sad ones can pull us back to happy, as they pass on by. I know just which essays to send him next.

I don't want to be hurt again. He needs to know that.

## Jocelyn And The Merry-Go-Round Horse
### Vancouver, British Columbia, 1992

"You'll like this one," says my six-year-old niece confidently. She hands me a thin volume from the stack of books on the wicker table near to us. I rifle the pages, immediately drawn to the brilliant-hued illustrations. Yes, this one suits us both: flying horses, a beckoning universe and a little girl who creates magic. Jocelyn and I snuggle up at one end of the deep-cushioned living-room couch and begin to read.

"Once upon a time ..." I read slowly, enjoying the warmth of my sister's house and the patter of rain on the windows behind us. Heads bent, bodies close, Jocelyn and I soar into midnight skies with Melanie and the merry-go-round horse. Our hands grasp the wind-tangled mane, our eyes shine with the reflection of countless stars. If we wanted, we could reach out and touch the moon and its edges would be as soft as a cotton quilt. Sky-travellers, safe on the back of a kind and happy creature who has traded wood and circles for the love of adventure in a child's smile. I smile, too, and think about Rory, the horse that I ride once a week, down along the banks of the Fraser River.

Rory had been standing in the rain for an hour when I went by the barn to see him today. His heavy winter coat was streaked with wetness and the hair on his neck and shoulders was curled and matted. I called to him and watched him consider the muddy path from his end of the paddock to where I stood, apple in hand. I rocked the apple in my palm. Rory whickered, swished his tail and ambled over. This horse is so big that I cannot touch the top of his back unless I stand on tiptoe; I can only touch his ears when he drops his head and submits to gentle pulls on their tear-drop shapes. There are days when I wish I could strike down the fences that border his life, set him free from the schedules of humans, but if he were wild, the small gift of an apple would not draw him close to me.

Last year I saw wild horses for the first time, in Alberta. Above their heads, a blue bowl of prairie sky; beneath their hooves, long grass and wildflowers. A thick-necked stallion stood a short distance from the herd. His dark, alert eyes did not move from the two human shapes on the edge of his world. One small move from us produced three small moves from the herd.

It was summer; the horses were fat and their coats shone from a rich diet of barley and clover. In winter, my friend said, when the snow piles high on the plains, you can count every rib on the horses' sides. That's when the native people, on whose land these horses graze, bring in bales of hay to keep them from starving. Some die anyway. But by the time the spring chinooks blow in, warm and constant, many foals are nestled close to the mares' sides. When it rains, or when the wind blows strong enough to buckle thin legs, the foals are nudged together and encircled by the bodies of the adult horses. Windsong blends with the howl of coyotes in the surrounding hills.

"Soon it would be morning. Melanie and the merry-go-round horse began the long journey down from the heavens. In another moment the sun would rise and Melanie would be back in her bed, about to begin a new day …" As we near the end of the story, I am aware of Jocelyn's slow, deep breathing and the heaviness of her head against my shoulder. She is not asleep – but very close. I pitch my voice low and read the last paragraph.

"But the merry-go-round horse could not return to the circle of horses at the carnival. He was no longer a wooden beast without movement, without feelings; he could not go back to his life before the magic. Melanie slipped off his back and ran across the ground to her house. She did not look or wave goodbye. She left the merry-go-round horse alone in the field, the steady rain mixing with his tears."

No. I must have missed something. There must be another page. Jocelyn is sitting up now and looking at me, hazel eyes full of concern. She knows the story well; she is not surprised by the ending. But she has heard my voice falter and senses that I have stopped breathing to prevent the tears from falling. She expects her aunt to say something adult and soothing, to pull back from the sodden field where a wingless pony stands alone.

"S'okay, Joss, I just thought …" That the merry-go-round horse would be cherished. That no one with the cloak of magic on their shoulders could reject the gift of loyalty. That love didn't have a time limit or disappear when the dagger in Orion's belt faded. That trust meant the exchange of care and protection. That a coyote's howl could not break the ranks of unity.

"… that the story would have a different ending."

Jocelyn hugs me fiercely. "Mommy cried, too, when she read it. Don't be sad. It's all right."

And in a moment, with Jocelyn's soft arms around my neck, it is all right. Tonight I am the magic horse, carrying Jocelyn into her cosy bedroom, where the nightlight glows and the shelves are crowded with books and toys.

I tuck her under the pastel-coloured quilt, kiss her and ask the question repeated every week since she was able to talk: "And how long shall I keep you?"

We chime the answer: *"For a million, trillion years – beyond forever."*

It is to this place I will take the merry-go-round horse. I will greet him with pockets full of fruit, and trace the star on his forehead with loving hands.

## SEA SONGS AND MOONLIGHT ON THE WATER
### – FOR F.V. FAN ISLE AND HER SKIPPER –
### PENDER HARBOUR, BRITISH COLUMBIA, 1993

"We have a wonderful view," says the restaurant owner, crossing the room to open the curtains on the western-facing wall. "You can see right to the end of the bay and beyond. To the ocean. I think you'll like it."

Jo-Ann and I follow, menus in hand.

At five o'clock in the afternoon, it's too early for dinner but not too early to consider whether or not to eat here later. The view may clinch the deal.

It's taken us a year to get here. Not to the restaurant, but to a place where three days belong to two old friends with a need for sea songs and moonlight on the water.

I forget how many times we've had to cancel this trip – don't want to think about it, either. We decided, when we left Vancouver yesterday, that all mention of work and finances was forbidden. What we want, in this place of forests and tides, is the time to slow our thoughts, and share them as we choose.

In the long sweep of harbour behind the curtains I see only one thing. For a few accelerated heartbeats my eyesight becomes impossibly keen. Hundreds of feet away from the troller, my vision records every detail of her classic West Coast style. Poles high, cabin low, the name painted sharp blue on a white stern.

"Fan Isle." The words are raven sounds, raw and uneven. They fly from my mouth, flutter against the glass pane. I turn to Jo-Ann, repeat the words, point out the window. "Don't you see her?"

Jo-Ann says something – I just can't hear her. But I can hear the tone of understanding and that's all that matters. She knows I'm going to bolt, that I must get away from these four walls, out and down to the wharf. Quickly, before the boat casts off and disappears into autumn sky and darkening waters.

The sun not quite set and the air already a chill wrap around neck, face and hands. Jogging down the steep paved road to the water I hear the steady smack of Jo-Ann's rubber-soled footsteps behind me.

A moment more and we'll be ...

The cabin door is closed, the decks bare. Rubber bumpers squeak against the wooden lip of the dock. No lights, or music or crackle from a VHF radio. Sitting high in the water, too: an empty hold, cleaned of fish and ice. Season's over.

I prepare myself for the worst – and it's not necessary: the vessel looks as good from close up as she did from far away. Tidy, clean and well-maintained. Decks could use an oiling but other than that, not bad. No, excellent.

I loved her best. Never hit really rough weather with her and wouldn't have worried if I had. Comfortable, a good sea boat, with that indefinable quality the fishermen call "fishy," as though the catch came aboard of its own volition, preferred the frigid confines of her belly to the wider toss of current and wave. When the boat sold, I couldn't transfer my allegiance to the bigger, more expensive vessel that took her place – a stubborn gift of loyalty, in return for the gift of safety she had provided.

"Of all the boats in the fleet to see ... up here in the middle of nowhere. She looks so good." I swipe at my cheeks with the back of my wrist, shake my hair into my face. "It's okay, we can go now."

Feather graze of hand touches my arm. "Take as long as you want," Jo-Ann says. "We're in no rush."

By the time we leave, every scupper space and davit curve is memorized again.

Later, when hunger comes, the hillside restaurant seems too high up from the bay. Instead we choose the waterside pub, which faces the harbour for pleasure vessels. Sleek, high-masted yachts in front of us as we sip cold Chablis and eat hot prawns and scallops, lemon squeezed over them.

The dozen or so lights on the float fingers come alight. Round, blue-tinged orbs, larger than the scattering of stars shining high above them. Larger and brighter still, the harvest moon, its valleys and craters etched dark on a golden surface. "Almost perfect," I say.

"Only one thing missing," says Jo-Ann.

"Ready to go?"

Four layers of clothing on now, making our way back down the tar-split road beside the commercial wharf. My guitar case is heavy, bumps my right leg, Jo-Ann's left leg, as we search for a place to align our shapes with the night shadows.

"Has to look west," I say. To watch the coppered ebb tide flowing.

"Has to be just right," says Jo-Ann. To enfold the rippling notes of music.

We reach the end of the road, circle back. Got to be here somewhere. A blue heron rises from the roof of a tool shed set midway on the float. It faces west, is tall enough to mute sound from the houses behind us. Bracing our backs against its frame we look directly across at my "fishy" friend.

"'Blue Moon' first?" I ask. Jo-Ann nods. My hands are stiff. I shake them, stir up the circulation, then press the tips to the strings. Can't strum with a pick, have to use my thumb – soft, keep it soft. For a gathering of three, the sea songs carry gently on the tide.

# 8

## *LEAP OF FAITH*

I've always cherished Don's unflappability. He may get owly now and again, to use an East Coast expression for being irritable, but unlike me, he doesn't go from zero to panic in a couple of heartbeats. Uncertain childhoods can do that to you. I don't know if I've seen Don actually panicked – a very good thing to say about a skipper and a husband. He also isn't given to moral indignation or lofty righteousness. If he were, I don't think we could have joined our lives. Like my dad once said, Don pretty much thinks people do the best they can, with the self-awareness and wisdom they have at any particular time. If I didn't believe that, too, I would never have achieved any self-forgiveness. It took me a long time to understand that self-forgiveness isn't a luxury, it's a necessity. Without it, you are a self-pitying, self-absorbed shell.

Don has never once thrown it in my face that I left a fiancé only weeks before we were to be married. Nor has he judged the reasons I did this. I left to be with another man, a Misguided Angel. That relationship almost obliterated my understanding of the twin birthrights of independent joy and self-respect. But I was going to Make It Right, Make It Work, however maimed I became in the process. If not, how could I live with the pain of leaving my fisherman? His sins, in retrospect, were venal, not mortal

– but his belligerently resistant ways were so terribly hard for me to understand. His "no" list was extensive: marriage; children; living in the city; dogs; smoking. Ten years of living strictly in the present with no plans for a future will wear down any woman, no matter how patient and optimistic. When the reluctant proposal of marriage was made, it was, as my mother intuited immediately, "Too little too late." After I left him, of course, his angel-halo shone brighter with each passing year. In the end, I didn't know who he was, angel or regular man. I still don't know.

After nine years together, there are layers of memories. Of these, three remain sharp: his big smile as he ran down the beach to meet me for the first time and to carry my heavy guitar case; the calloused, strong hands that killed fish with an exquisite economy; a skin that smelled faintly like fruit, set just beyond reach. I have not the smallest notion how he remembers me.

Apart from his stubborn ways, my fisherman was one of the kindest and most generous people I have known. He celebrated any success I had with a jubilant heart. My sadnesses, on the other hand, were foreign lands to him. As far as I know, he never knew why I left. Like any cheating spouse, I didn't want him to know I'd cheated and then chosen someone else over him. I thought keeping quiet was the most honourable thing to do. I desperately didn't want to hurt or shame him for a single minute, let alone a lifetime. My own shame was crippling, made eating almost impossible for over five years. For all I know, it was more painful for him for the breakup to be so inexplicable. God knows he lost weight after I left, too.

I never loved him more than the day I left him. The love was so big it was like tripping up a mountain, with a huge backpack on, never getting near the top. But I left anyway. The Misguided Angel said *Believe*, as the fisherman never had, and *I believed*, as I never had.

I was haunted for many years by the last time I saw my fisherman at the apartment we lived in, which I had left months before. He offered me a supper of chicken stew. He'd cooked it a à la fisherman, in a pressure cooker. It smelled rich and wonderful.

Every cell in my body told me that I wasn't fit to sit down with him and break bread. Every cell in his body radiated the need for me to stay, to do just that. I told him I had to go and gently pulled the apartment door closed behind me. Outside the door I doubled over holding my gut. Wicked, it was wicked to deny him that one small request. But I could not do it, could not be near all that sorrowing gentleness without doing something savage. I don't even know what that means, really. I'd felt so diminished by him over the years, so disrespected and patronized. To realize that those feelings didn't matter, that I'd always love him, if only for those killing hands, was one of the most defeating moments of my life. It didn't matter that I'd said no, at last. He still won.

You always want these huge life moments to make perfect sense later on. But if life is a series of "later ons" as we age, then "perfect sense" must change over the years, too. The sense I have now, imperfect though it may be, is that the courage to love is incremental, uniquely new each time it graces our lives, but built on the foundation of other, earlier loves. These can be romantic loves, familial loves or the loves we share with friends or animal companions. Frightened or not, there are moments our hearts are capable of making huge leaps of faith. Hearts need to do this, or they wither and life goes monochrome. But without the history that goes before these leaps, without the love, loss and fury of those other times, there wouldn't be the ability to leap yet again … just a little higher. Each incarnation of love will disappoint and hurt us at some point; like the scorpion, love's nature is to wound. The flip side of love is joy, though. It's a package deal.

Of course my fisherman didn't really win anything except a broken heart, in those early months after I left. Nor did I lose, all those years ago. While the Misguided Angel only believed in us for a short while and in a mirror of my life, departed badly – I had time, then, to think about all the qualities I hoped for in a life-mate – and the ones I would never again compromise on. When I answered the phone in May 1996 and said hello to Don, I didn't know it, but the journey toward love had begun again – a love of greater depth and peace. No more guilt and sadness – the future beckoned fresh as a nor'westerly over Pacific waters.

*God grant me the serenity to accept the things I cannot change,*
*The courage to change the things I can,*
*And the wisdom to know the difference.*

The AA Serenity Prayer, which Dad repeated often over a lifetime, as do I, though I am not a member of AA. The prayer works for all, I believe, if you can live, not merely recite, the words.

Serenity. Courage. Wisdom. And forgiveness, of every sort. It is through this lens I do my best to look backward and live forward.

# 9

## THE PFO LETTER

*JUNE 1996, VANCOUVER, BRITISH COLUMBIA*

So if I can't do this – have a romantic relationship with Silver Donald Cameron – then how do we go on from here? We've been talking almost every evening for nearly two months. We've mailed one another countless essays and books. Now we're on this new thing called e-mail and sending one another at least two messages a day electronically – not that I am very good at that process yet. Why does he have to bring sex into all this? Why do *we* have to bring sex into all this?

    Because he likes you. Because you like him, too. Because it's what happens when attraction and trust and enjoyment and laughter walk hand and hand into the same room. But we're not in the same room! He's in Cape Breton and I am in Vancouver. He's a widower with a hamburger heart and I am only just functioning after that last brutal round in the ring called love. I don't want to do this – and there isn't even an actual *place* to do this! Here I am, an adult "child" of thirty-seven living with my retired schoolteacher mother, doing my damnedest to make more money as a freelance writer. Ah gee, Mum, do you think we could borrow the house for a day or two so we can have a little privacy ... joking, joking, dear God, I *am* joking and dear God, *no,* I can't bear these indignities – makes me all squirmy and frantic just thinking about it. A hotel room would be icy and bizarre. So that takes care of my end of the country. As for his end, I am not flying four thousand miles to a place I don't know at all, to a man I don't know, not really, just for sex. If we ever get to that point, it will damn well be on home turf for me, if it means a literal patch of West Coast dirt or sand.

I have an article deadline. I just want to go to the barn and go for a hack on Kaber, my sweet-faced half-Arabian gelding. Maybe I can do that now, and work on the article this evening.

Anything to put off the inevitable.

Do I really have to write this dear and lovely man another PFO letter? What would I say this time, anyway?

## June 1996, Isle Madame, Cape Breton

Dear Marjorie

Your e-mail was waiting for me when I logged online this morning. I could tell you I am surprised by its contents, but I am not. You've been circling around to this for some days.

"An interesting and distinguished man," you say, "with whom it has been a privilege to converse and share the stories of our lives." I would happily lose some of this loftiness for the opportunity of closer times with you. However, I respect your decision and won't ask again for us to meet face to face. If you do change your mind – *as you did once before* – I am one phone call or e-mail away. I can be on a plane with one day's notice.

You say that, among other things, you are uneasy with my having contacted you so early after the loss of Lulu. It is important to me that you understand why I did this. From earlier comments you'd made, I knew you were single. For all I knew, that status could have changed at any time. I didn't want to hesitate and lose you – *all for the sake of some misplaced sense of bourgeois propriety.*

I think you are wrong, by the way, if such a word can be politely used to describe this final change of course you've decided on. I think we could have an astonishing time together as lovers and even, possibly, an astonishing life together. We are both people of the water; I can imagine so easily the different seas we could sail over, on my sailboat, *Silversark*. We could even sail to the Bahamas, as I told you I've always wanted to do. You always told me you envisioned more adventures in an already adventurous life. You also said you were tired of looking for love, wanted, instead, for someone to "drop from the sky."

*Marjorie, I am that which dropped from the sky.*

Thank you for sharing your essays with me, and all the e-mails – what a conversation it has been! There was one e-mail in particular that will stay with me always, about you and Kaber and riding alongside the Fraser – do you remember? You wrote me and said, "I rode my horse in the pouring rain, and cried for a woman I'd never met, and for the man who'd loved and lost her." You cried for Lulu and me – I was so moved. That's when I knew I had met someone special, and wanted to know you better. We will meet in person again sometime, I am sure. It won't be as I had envisioned the meeting, but I'll look forward to it all the same. I've enjoyed every moment of our talks and shared writings these past weeks. You are a lovely, blithe spirit and gifted writer. Keep on writing and keep on loving. You will be cherished again.

With respect and affection,

Don

## June 1996, Vancouver, British Columbia

Dear Don

You have respectfully done exactly what I asked you to do – gently back off – so why do I feel *utterly bereft*? I knew I depended on the regularity and warmth of our correspondence, but I really didn't understand how much. My days are quiet and cool again, not lit with the liveliness and warmth of your messages and phone calls. Even going to the barn to be with Kaber doesn't make me quite as happy as it did even a week ago, when I could look forward to telling you all about my riverside rambles. I have so much to tell you about Kaber-boy shenanigans this week!

There was also another essay I wanted to share with you, about another horse I used to ride, an Appaloosa named Boo. I've been staring at the fax machine for an hour, wishing I could send it to you. But what have I gone and done? I've said no phone calls and no writing exchanges for a bit, so we can reclaim our regular lives again.

Why did I say this? What is so special about our regular, solitary lives? No one makes me laugh like you do – except maybe my siblings and you haven't met them yet! You should meet my older brother and sister. They would enjoy you! So would my little sisters, my niece, my nephews. You should meet all my family. I should meet yours. They sound like wonderful, warm people. We should eat sockeye salmon together, not just talk about it. I want you to come to my barn and see Kaber. I want to walk those riverside trails with you. Not so long from now, the blackberry bushes along the trails will be heavy with fruit. We can pick a bucket and eat them, sitting on big rocks at the river's edge, watching the tugs and barges go by.

Do you think we could do some of these things? And oh my God, you haven't even met Leo yet. You haven't spent time with a whippet, a true and wondrous whippet – you poor man! You do not know – I mean you truly do not know, because it must be experienced – what joy a whippet creates, just by breathing.

Maybe we could talk and write just a little bit more … before we got together? Do you think that would be all right?

*Misplaced sense of bourgeois propriety* – a bit brutal, perhaps, but I understand.

I can't stand it. I am sending you the essay on Boo. He was cared for by two sisters – just like Karin and I cared for Coqeyn. They never lost their way, though. That was important for me to see – can you understand? I guess I still believe in magic – it's my fatal flaw. But I think you do, too. Who wants a life with no shivers and shimmers?

I told my brother Geoffrey that I couldn't go forward with you. We were having a coffee at a Starbucks on Commercial Drive, after a hike on the North Shore Mountains yesterday. He gets this bland look on his face sometimes, when he wants to say a lot but doesn't, figures it's better for me to get to an idea on my own. The look drives me nuts; it's like we're little kids again and I can't keep up to his longer strides when we're walking, but he won't cut me any slack. It's like *You got legs, use them*. Except this time it's like *Well, you got a brain, use it*. And all he actually said was: "Tell me again why you don't want to know this man better?" I didn't really have an answer. Then he cracked a joke, said, "I'd have to tell the guy, good luck getting my sister out of B.C.! Maybe it's for the best you don't get involved with him."

I smiled – it was funny – but I didn't like that last bit. Ah hell, do you think maybe we could we talk later in the day? I've been wanting to share this essay about Boo with you for ages.

With affection,
Marjorie

# 10

## A Matter Of Trust

### Guarding The Skyline
### Vancouver, British Columbia, 1992

A friend of mine moved to the country two weeks ago. For the past year, he and I have spent nearly every Sunday afternoon together. We have shared wild weather and wilder moods and I will miss his good company. But "Boo" the Appaloosa has something now which I never knew he needed, never guessed he longed for, never imagined was as necessary to his health as clean water and a warm bran mash: an unobscured skyline.

Boo and I are probably the same age. I am thirty-two and he has been twenty-five for some years now. I think of him as a seasoned warrior, a kind-hearted "packer" who never caused me a moment of alarm or discomfort in the entire year I rode him. I trusted him, completely, the way I used to trust my Arab/Welsh pony, Coqeyn, who I owned when I was a teenager. When I started leasing Boo, owned by two sisters, Tash and Letsa, I told myself not to get too attached. I am old enough to know how wrenching final goodbyes to animals can be. And you never know when those goodbyes will come along. I would love my roany, spotted Boo so much, and no more.

We would walk, he and I, for many hours on our Sunday rendezvous. Usually we went up into the UBC Endowment Lands; occasionally, when the weather was warm, as far down as Foreshore Beach, across the harbour from downtown Vancouver.

Boo loved going to the beach. His energy and endurance were amazing. He'd fly over logs as though he were on a hunt and his flat-out gallop over the firm sands used to make me feel as though we were co-pilots, breaking the sound barrier. He could go forever, it seemed; it was me, legs shaking and face streaked with wind-tears and ocean spray, who would rein him back to a slower gait. No horse I ever knew galloped as big and bold as Boo did. His strides demolished the distances.

Boo arrived at his new home on a cold November afternoon. Perhaps he thought he was being trucked to a show – in early years, he had showed Open Jumper and Prix St. Georges-level dressage – or perhaps he knew, with each bumpy mile from Southlands to Langley, that his life was mysteriously changing. Whatever he sensed, he stepped down from the big commercial truck in his usual calm way. Looking quietly around him, he saw a house, a barn and a four-acre field framed on three sides by other fields.

At first it didn't seem so strange or out of the ordinary to him. He and the three other horses he'd trucked out with did all the regular things horses do when they realize they have lots of room to move out: gallop, buck, bicker and graze. After a half-hour or so they settled down to concentrate on the grass. All except Boo, that is. Boo took himself to the farthest corner of the field, planted his hooves perfectly square and stood motionless. He fixed his eyes on the western horizon and didn't move – for two hours. Once in a long while, his head would turn; for five or ten minutes he would contemplate the southern horizon, then back to the west. He stood giraffe-tall, ears pricked. Every muscle in his body guarded the beauty of a winter skyline.

Boo did not want to come into the barn at feeding time. The sky glowed orange and mauve, night had sharpened the air – and still he hadn't moved. It was as though he'd kept the landscape from moving through the force of will held in his steady gaze. Maybe he thought that if he moved, the expanse of ground and sky would shrink, and he'd be back at Southlands, surrounded by paddocks, houses and cars. Fifteen years of living on The Flats. A decade and a half without a 360-degree view of the world.

I led him into the barn in near-darkness. The electricity in the barn had not been connected yet – there were no lights – and so he hesitated at the door of his stall, unable to see if the ground was level. One hoof went out tentatively. I bumped my shoulder against his: "S'okay, Boo, in you go."

Maybe it was the way he trusted me when I asked him to step into his new stall, even though his cataracts make it impossible for him to see much anymore. Maybe it was a sudden memory of him rounding the corner of a forest path, seeing a fallen Douglas fir ahead and with one word from me, transforming into an airborne locomotive. Maybe it was the sound of his dull old teeth working so hard on his grain. Or maybe it was the alert expression on his face as he turned away from his food and watched me walk out of the barn to my car. All I knew was that I couldn't see either. *I said I'd love you this much and no more.*

"Come out whenever you want," said Letsa warmly.

"Ride as often as you want," said a smiling Tash. "His eyesight's fine in the day."

Two kind and close sisters, with a love of animals that bound them closer yet.

I nodded, though I wasn't sure what I actually said. With luck, I said thank you. I'll say it again, just in case: Thank you. Someone just said, "See you soon," so I'll say that, too. Great new place, I added, congratulations on your new home. The horses will be so happy here – all that glorious, wide-open space.

As I drove away, the image in my mind of a tall, shaggy Appaloosa guarding the skyline stayed with me. *That sky won't go anywhere. Trust me.* The way I trusted you.

## JULY 1996, VANCOUVER, BRITISH COLUMBIA

I am so confused, and so wary of trusting. I don't think I can do this. Maybe being alone is easier.

# 11

## THE RENDEZVOUS

*AUGUST 1996, VANCOUVER, BRITISH COLUMBIA*

What else could I do? He said he was going to drive out to the coast in a Winnebago, put up a sign on our front lawn that read: "Marjorie won't go out with me; Marjorie is being mean," and leave it there for all the neighbours in the townhouse complex to read, day after endless day – until I did go out with him. It would be easy to say he was kidding – but I really don't think he was. If I've learned anything since that first phone call back in April, it's that Silver Donald Cameron is a cheerful but cussedly stubborn man – who will not, absolutely will not take no for an answer.

And I am glad! This is it, no more shilly-shallying around. After six months of talking, letters, sharing our writings and over eight hundred e-mails, Silver Donald Cameron and Marjorie Simmins are going on a face-to-face date! He'll be here in a couple of days – so much to do first! We are going to stay down at his family's cottage in Point Roberts, Washington. Point Roberts, can you imagine! That's where my friends and I went all the time I was a teenager, to dance at The Breakers nightclub. The music was fantastic, live bands and big names from all over the U.S. Nowdays, I go to The Reef tavern with my girlfriends to play pool on Sunday afternoons. I wonder if Don plays pool? I hope so.

I love rustic and weird Point Roberts. It's like a fingertip of the United States, surrounded entirely by Canada. When they drew the 49th parallel, they just lopped off the very tip of The Point and declared it was American land. The school kids have to be bussed back through Canada and then back into the States again, at the Peace Arch border crossing, just to go to school each day. More than anything, The Point is Canadian summer-cottage country. It should be a part of Canada, for heaven's sake. Instead it's stuck off by itself, with Canada to its north and Washington State proper across the Salish Sea to the south. Americans and Canadians call Point Roberts "Dogpatch U.S.A." It's one of the poorest parts of America, with almost everyone on assistance during the winter and not enough jobs to go around even in the summer. Well, of course, it's in complete isolation from the rest of the country. There are some hockey-player mansions now, over by the yacht club, but in general, people live modestly. And no industry, of any sort, though there used to be fish canneries there. That's why it's so peaceful to drive to on a sunny Sunday afternoon.

Anyway, turns out Don's parents bought a place down there in the '40s. Don's youngest brother Ken owns the cottage now. What a perfect place for a first visit. Quiet, green, away from prying eyes and eager ears. All those pretty paths through the woods and the endless tidal flats at Boundary Bay for Leo to run on –

*Oh dear.* How do I explain that the dog sleeps with me every night? Does he really like dogs – or did he just say that to make polite noises? I am not going anywhere without Leo. No way. If things go strange for any reason, me and my mutt will just hop in my trusty Celica and drive away –

*(– one, two, three; three, two, one –)*

I'm not scared – I'm just very nervous and keyed up. I wish both families didn't know every detail of this story! But there's no way to hide it after all this time. My oldest sister Zoë actually sent Don an e-mail saying that the whole Simmins family was in favour of a rendezvous between Don and me. All the grown-ups, anyway. I haven't told my little sisters and my niece much in the way of detail;

that can come later, if at all. Heaven knows how this is all going to pan out.

*(– five, six, seven; seven, six, five –)*


AUGUST 1996, MORNING.
THE CAMERON FAMILY COTTAGE,
POINT ROBERTS, WASHINGTON STATE


I brought lots of groceries, of course; that's who I am, someone who likes to cook for other people. My whole family is like that, except poor Mum, who got really tired cooking for all of us for so many years. My oldest sister pitched in for a while and then my brother Geoffrey and I did a fair bit of the cooking through our high school years. Mum loved that! She loves it now, that I do all the cooking for us at home. Least I can do, for the love and sanctuary she's given me.

*Mum, I am scared. I said I wasn't but I am. I don't know what to do next – this is all so intimate and overwhelming –*

Don enjoyed his breakfast – which wasn't fancy, only bacon and eggs and toast, with good thick-cut marmalade and a bowl of local raspberries. He's started right in on the dishes, which is nice. That's the rule in our family: whoever cooks doesn't have to clean up. So I am glad he's good with that. I was delighted to see him come off the plane with live lobsters in hand. We cooked them last night, for our first evening together here at the cottage. I had no clue how to actually eat a whole lobster; I've done this maybe once in my life and that was years ago. Don found some nutcrackers and sharp skinny knives and one way or another, watching how he did it, I managed to get the meat out of the shell. It was delicious. *Hope you enjoy your first taste of the Maritimes*, he smiled, and we toasted another glass of wine.

*All right, I drank too much wine and tequila – Dutch courage and all that – and that's partly why I feel so off-kilter. But that's only part of it. So much time being theoretical lovers ... and now we are real lovers. Do I look different? I feel different. Really different. Good different. Like spending the night in a curling tropical wave: everything*

*turquoise and rushing and warm all around us. We should have stayed
in the wave, not come out to this morning-cold kitchen with polite
queries for salt and pepper, please, and would you like more coffee?*

(– eleven, twelve, thirteen; fourteen, fifteen, sixteen –)

"I am feeling a bit funny …," I say to Don.

"Really?" says Don. "Tell me about it." He has just dried his
hands on a tea towel and has retrieved his half-full coffee cup from
the counter. He settles himself in the white wicker chair by the
French doors, which look out to the front yard. He is dressed in
summer cottons, dappled by sunlight. I like looking at him.

"I'm sorry," I say. "I don't want to spoil things. I just feel very
vulnerable and on edge."

Don takes a sip of his coffee. "What can we do about that?"

What can *we* do about that? Is that what he said – *we*? What
a novel concept. I don't know what to say. Oh God, you silly girl,
don't start crying.

I clear my throat. "Uh, well, I guess I just have one way of
doing these things. When I feel funny I like to be outside … in
the sun … with Leo – preferably by the water. Could we do that?"
My heart is pounding. If he doesn't want to do this, I'll have to go
anyway –

He is laughing! Why?

"That dog is hilarious! He was right under the covers on your
side of the bed last night. Is that where he usually sleeps?"

I nod, rapidly.

Don looks around the kitchen. "He's had his breakfast but he's
not – is that where he is now?"

I nod again.

"He'd stay there all day, wouldn't he?"

"He's a whippet," I say, willing him to understand a breed he
knows nothing about, "a sighthound. Two speeds, stop and go." We
are both laughing now.

"All right," says Don, "then let's see him go." He is picking up
his camera from the counter by the telephone. "Boundary Bay it is,
stateside."

My heart is hurting with happiness. It hurts just a bit more when I glance outside and see a sun-bright summer morning against an aqua sky. "Watch this," I say. "Leeeee-oh! Let's go for a walk!"

*Ker-thump.* Four tidy whippet paws land together on the floor in the bedroom. *Whappety-whap.* Two ears are shaken vigorously. *Clickety-clickety-clickety.* Many claw tips, which should have been clipped last week, or even the week before, are rapidly tapping against the linoleum floors. We turn to see a tan and white hound come trotting into the kitchen. His eyes are the darkest of browns, backlit by humour and life joy. He looks like a small deer. He stretches long and low, his way of "putting on his hat" to go outside. The movements are also similar to an athlete warming up.

I feel a shiver of excitement. Don has never seen a whippet run. Pound for pound, whippets are the fastest animal on earth. This will be just as fun for me to watch. Even though I've seen Leo run flat-out hundreds of times, I'll see it again today for the first time, through Don's eyes. With luck it will be low tide at the beach. Nothing Leo loves more than caroming through tidals pools, water pluming out on either side of him. We'll take a tennis racket to smack a ball for him to retrieve. That will really get him flying. I can't wait to see Don's reaction to all that speed, grace and beauty.

I pocket my car keys and perch my sunglasses on my head. Don and Leo go out the door. Pausing to find my purse, I watch them saunter companionably towards my Toyota Celica. A man and a hound, walking at the same easy pace, breathing the same soft summer air. I have the strangest feeling that I am watching my forever world in a single, sunlit moment.

## 12

# FOREVER WORLDS

## ILLEGALLY CUTE
### D'ESCOUSSE, NOVA SCOTIA, 2003

"I swear, you have a heart of stone." My husband's pronouncement is softened by an amused tone and a conniving smile. But he's not through with me yet: "How can you resist *that*?"

"That" is a minuscule collection of puppy parts – tail tip, two front paws, one floppy ear, the rest obscured by a blanket – which is officially known as Chancey, the baby beagle. A miniature baby beagle, if you please. Didn't know they even made them that small. It is illegally cute. Which hardens my heart more.

"Out of the question," I reply. "They dig. They bay. They dismember small, furry creatures, with great skill and high glee. Utterly intractable." I shake my head vigorously. "No, we are a beagle-free family."

"But we don't have to be," he wheedles, "do we?"

There are appropriate times (alone) and bad times (audience) for spousal arguments. If you choose the latter, as we are commencing to do on this muggy Nova Scotia evening, pitch your voice low, and hope no one follows the exchanges. So far, so good. Chancey's owners are too busy being hospitable to us and cheery with one another to notice the drop in volume at our end of the kitchen table.

These are new friends. I wouldn't want them to misunderstand, or feel I am slighting their unquestionably dear addition to their family. After all, I am batty about most dogs, and battier yet about our own Leo, The Wonder Whippet.

It is the trend in my husband's thinking that has me on edge. They say wives are always the last to know – or is that believe? – the truth. I am proving the adage, having seen and ignored the warning signs for a long time now. At this moment the sign is neon-bright in my mind: my husband is a late-developing Small Dog Guy. This way madness … is guaranteed. At the very least, small dogs often represent Unique Challenges To Everyday Serenity. I close my eyes for a moment, resisting the panic that has somehow come to the granite organ in my chest.

"Later," I whisper. "We will discuss this later."

Thinking back, I can isolate the first indication of small-dog mania. Downtown Vancouver, May 2002, Hornby Street and Pacific Avenue.

"Omagodlook." Four words exhaled as one, but I got the drift, especially since my husband's arm shot out in front of us, his index finger pointing to an elongated bundle of wavy hair rapidly travelling east on Hornby. Straight towards us.

"Long-hair dachshund." In the tone of, We Must Have.

Sausage-dog, I thought, which is what we called them when I was a kid. Aloud, even then flinty-hearted: "Hairy wiener dog."

But my husband was already down on his knees on the pavement, his oohs and ahhs clearly audible to me, despite standing twenty feet back from the lovefest. In short order my husband collected relevant details on the turbocharged shoebox: name and location of breeder; lifespan, potential health and temperament concerns; cost and availability. The information, he told me, eyes evangelically alight, matches his earlier research on the breed.

*Earlier research?*

Well, all right, we had had, a few weeks prior, some discussions on Another Dog. Leo (have I mentioned he is the perfect dog?), twelve this past summer, has received strict orders to live forever. He will do his best for us, we know. But two of my lifelong girlfriends (one a breeder of English pointers, another a trainer and dog sports competitor) actually "stack" their canine family members. Thus, when the unbearable occurs, it is borne not in a suddenly dogless house, but in one that continues to have yips, saliva-strewn squeaky toys and bountiful hair on the couches. In this scenario, the heart mends – imperfectly, but sooner, say my friends. I know they are right – it is heart-logical – but I've only ever been one-dog monogamous. (All right, I've only ever had one dog of my very own. Doesn't affect his perfect status.)

"Great for the boat," continues my husband, as we left the street-scene love-a-thon. "One lap around the deck and he'd be done for the day. I could even design a shoulder bag to put him in, for easy loading – yeah, that could work … "He fell silent, working on the details of his design.

No response from me, only the instant mental image of a sausage-dog sandwich, tiny head out one end, mouse-tail out the other, body leather-encased.

"Please," I said, "I don't think I can handle this conversation."

The memories are piling up. The week before Christmas, also last year. We were decorating the tree. Work done for the day, seasonally sweet baking smells filling the house. "Joy to the World" on the CD player. Lovely tranquil moods, both of us.

Then: "Did I ever tell you my brother had Yorkies?"

Yorkshire terriers. In league with Satan for maelstrom and auditory chaos. They not only dig – for real and imagined rats – they climb. Pant legs. Pitched roofs. Your neighbour Christina, twitchy around dogs anyway, always dressed in crisp whites.

"Ye-es?" Frowning, angel in hand, I refocused on the tree, having totally lost the ideal spot I'd intended to hang it. Christmas, in a heartbeat, transformed into *such a chore.*

"I know they're ridiculously small – more like a floor mop than a dog – but they're kind of nice, too."

"Your point?"

"Oh, no point. 'Cept you did say you liked the Taylors' Yorkie, remember?"

Clarabelle. Affectionate, nominally obedient. But so tiny! What if you accidentally stepped on her – bird-bones wrapped in silken tresses. Think of the sound that would –

"Dog by dog sort of thing," I allowed, shuddering. "Some you like, some you don't. Just like people. I like the Taylors, too. But maybe not their great-aunt Bertha."

"Well, you seem awfully hard on small dogs generally. No need, really." His expression was so bland, so natural, innocent.

*My God! How blind could I be? He's been laying the groundwork for years!*

"What do you think of Chancey?" Our host's question pulls me back – slow, resistant, like taffy spooned up from a bowl – to the convivial kitchen we and Chancey's owners are gathered in.

I look up to see yet another man's eyes lit with religious dog-fervour. And puppy-fervour, the most dangerous, detached from common sense. In lieu of an answer, I smile, then look down on the current floor tableau, puppy belly and puppy snout, both offered up for adoration. Leo, sleeping deeply on the same blanket, dreaming, perhaps, of borderless terrain and four young-again legs, to carry him like wind over water. His tan and white body, elegant in motion and repose, has always made me think of a deer. So, too, his eyes, amber-dark, warm with intelligence and humour. But he is named for his lion-heart, which only in year twelve has started to falter. *Remember the deal, Leo. Live forever.*

A gargle of baby-beagle snores rises in the air. A six-inch puppy leg twitches. My rock-heart shatters, re-forms in softer form, as it will another day, forever from now.

"He's perfect," I say. "Aren't they all?"

## THE DAYS OF THREE FOREVER
### HAMPTON, VIRGINIA, APRIL 2006

SDC:

*Seven in the morning, and I cradle thirty-eight pounds of whippet in my left arm as I carefully climb from the boat to the dock. I have lifted Leo on and off the boat more than 1,200 times since he and Marjorie and I sailed from Cape Breton in July, 2004. We have sailed 4,500 miles together.*

*He has had a terrible night, his breath trembling, his heartbeat chaotic, his frail body unable to lie in comfort. I carry him a few steps, and he gives a little twist. Put me down, he is saying, I want to walk. I carefully set him on his feet, and he trots jauntily up the wharf – ears up, head high, a dog on a mission.*

*He jumps down the two wooden steps to the grass, does his business, and then stands very still, eyes narrowed, sniffing the air, orienting himself in the new day. Ah, yes. Birdsong, and the smell of fish. I'm in Hampton, Virginia. I have friends in these shore-side townhouses. Fine.*

*He turns back toward the dock. At the steps, he halts. Help me, he is saying, I can't manage this. He is two months short of his fifteenth birthday, and he has arthritis, congestive heart disease, fatty tumours, cataracts and hearing loss. He is not the light-hearted, speeding bullet of a dog that he was when I met him, a decade ago.*

*I lift him, and carry him down the dock to the boat. And this time he doesn't object.*

MLS:

The small house in Fort Langley, B.C., had a river of baby whippets flowing through it. There were three, four, no, five of them falling off couches and tumbling together on the carpeted floors. There were so many plump puppy limbs tangled together, I couldn't tell one animal from another.

"Jocelyn," I whispered to my five-year-old niece, who stood in quivering delight by my side, "how will we ever choose the right one?" It was 1991, I was thirty-two years old, and had never had my very own dog. My heart thudded. This was a *forever choice*.

Thump, *ker-smack*, thump. It sounded as though someone had vigorously rolled a five-pound bag of potatoes down the staircase that led to the living room. Instead, we turned to see a sixth puppy careening around a corner toward us. His body, like the others, was short-backed and ended in a wind-milling tail. Unlike the others, this one had a pronounced black mask on his white face. He hurled his tan and white body onto the puppy pile of his siblings.

"That's Bandit," laughed the woman into whose home we had come. She was a full-time equestrian judge and a part-time breeder of dogs. "Just his kennel name, but I couldn't call him anything else with a mask like that, could I?"

Perhaps not, but I could. I wanted my dog to live up to his name, not settle down to it. I didn't want a thieving dog, no matter how cute the name. I wanted a dog who would be a co-adventurer, with a heart as big and brave as a – lion. Leonine. *Leo.* That's what I'd call him.

Bandit streaked by us. Jocelyn and I locked eyes. *Yes.*

From that day on, there was never any reason for me to be apart from Leo. Two weeks earlier, I'd quit a salaried job and begun working at home as a freelance writer. When I worked at my computer, Leo snoozed on a nearby couch. When I drove hither and yon to do interviews or take photos, Leo came with me, and waited in the car.

When the work day was done, we'd hightail it to the many paths and parks alongside the Fraser River, or to the lowlands of Vancouver's Southlands, where I rode horses and Leo revelled in being a barn-hound. On weekends we'd

Leo the Wonder Whippet, mid-air in a field above the village of D'Escousse, Nova Scotia, 1998. (Photo by Silver Donald Cameron.)

Leo, Don and Marjorie on their wedding day, March 14, 1998, at the Unitarian Church, in Vancouver, B.C.

hike the North Shore mountain trails or drive to Whistler Mountain. I'd pack a picnic for us – sandwiches for me, canned food for him – and we'd find a pretty waterside spot to have our lunch along the way.

His mask had faded. But his mercury-glinting eyes were still thickly outlined with black, like a kohl-eyed Egyptian of long ago. *Friends share,* said those expressive eyes. I wasn't very good at being strict.

"All right, all right. Egg salad or chicken?"

Once I took him bushwacking near Pender Harbour, north of Vancouver. No trail, only a thick latticework of sword ferns and the high starbursts of uprooted deadfall. Leo threw himself at these immense, felled Douglas firs. If not for their sodden, crumbling sides, he would have scrambled up and jumped clear. He submitted to my help – a gut-wrenching heave over the top – though not before I could prevent numerous ill-fated leaps of his own. When the day was over, I cried to see his bloodied belly.

Leo thought the steaks that night were just fine.

And so we worked, lived and played in Richmond, B.C., a contented duo surrounded by family and friends. There was no reason to change anything, unless the change suited us both very well.

"A whippet?" asked a wonderful man I'd just begun corresponding and talking with in 1996. "I've never seen a whippet. What are they like?"

Where did I start? And how to say, love me, love my ... "They're like a greyhound, except smaller," I answered inadequately. "They're so ..." Long pause.

"Hello? Are you still there?"

"Well, they're so wholehearted about everything. Everything you can do is just more fun with a whippet. They love the world so much, they make you love it more, too." I closed my eyes and saw Leo as I'd seen him earlier that day, on the beach. "When you see him run, your heart hurts. It's that beautiful."

I didn't tell him, then, how soft a whippet's ears are – like a chamois cloth – and how sadness can be banished by holding a whippet close. These discoveries came to him later.

When Don and I married in 1998, Leo had spring flowers interwoven in his collar. He and many other dogs belonging to friends thronged into the church's courtyard after the wedding. Leo found us for a brief, reassuring moment, then whirled away back into the crowd.

The days of three forever had begun.

SDC:

*Nine in the morning, and two gentle, kind women are aboard the boat – a veterinarian and her assistant, recommended by friends. For the first time ever, Leo did not jump out of the berth to greet his visitors. He is utterly spent, too weary to stand. The vet confirms what we already knew. His vital signs are very feeble.*

*But he comes sharply alert when Marjorie produces four strips of bacon. We take turns breaking them up and feeding them to him – a feast of bacon, the most bacon he has ever seen. He wolfs it down eagerly.*

*I pick him up and stretch him out on a towel on the galley table. He raises his head in momentary consternation, but lies down when we ask him to. I hold his head, gazing into his eyes, telling him how he is loved. Marjorie wraps her arms around his body, muttering Thank you, Thank you, over and over. The vet lifts his foreleg and slips a needle into a vein.*

*Nothing happens. His eyes don't flicker, his body doesn't twitch. He just lies there, with his eyes half-open. The vet slips a hand under his leg.*

*"He's gone," she says. The two women leave us with the mortal remains of our gallant companion. The days of weeping begin.*

*Nine-thirty in the morning. I lift Leo from the table. The vet positions his limp neck across my shoulder. His head hangs down my back. He does not feel like Leo at all. Blinded by tears, I carry him up the wharf for the second time this morning.*

*And for the very last time, ever.*

## ANYTHING BUT BLUE. BUT SERIOUSLY CONFUSED.
### SEPTEMBER 1996, VANCOUVER, BRITISH COLUMBIA

If I thought I felt bereft when I had, weeks earlier, asked Don to stop phoning and writing me – and he had, promptly and respectfully – I could barely take in how disoriented and lonely I felt now, after our week-long visit in Point Roberts. He was once again home in Cape Breton, and I was once again home in Richmond. I have an acute imagination. It is possible, I thought, meandering along a pebbled dyke pathway by the Sturgeon Banks, Leo padding beside me, that I dreamed up the week – imagined the crescendos and tenderness. An affectionate e-mail from Don mere hours after he had arrived back in Nova Scotia assured me that *no, you didn't dream it.*

But then how could it be that I couldn't see his slim frame beside me, reach out to take his hand as we both walked along that pathway? Had I brought him to this wondrous place of river and sea, herons, songbirds and salmon, at the mouth of the Fraser? No, there hadn't been time to come here. I felt a quick press of pain to think it could be months – maybe years – before I could share this favourite spot at Steveston's westernmost corner with Don.

*Sharing.* It can be wondrous, too.

*Well, well? Tell all,* said friends and family members, beaming, relentless – *how did it go?* Fine, good, amazing, yes, *oh my yes,* you bet, seemed so right, no, really, I don't know what comes next – different people got different snippets and that was about all I was up to sharing. Small cyclones of confusion whirled across my mind, their winds taunting and contradictory. I think I could love him, yes; but move from B.C., no! You can do this, I know you can; no I can't – *really.* You need to do this, you know you do; what, need to jump off a cliff (as a good friend blithely said it would feel like to her), is that what I really need? Can't can't can't just too hard – but God, I miss him. What do I do now?

I write him: "Dear SDC – I have always had an adventurous life and expected that to continue. But I never thought someone would up the ante this much. I miss you. Yours in agitation and (probably) love, M."

"Dear MLS – Doesn't your dad always talk about one day at a time? Well, let's just do that, you and me. No need to think about all our tomorrows today. All you need to know today is that I, too, am missing you and hoping you will come to Cape Breton in October, as we discussed. The autumn leaves are stunning and we'll drive around the Cabot Trail, have some lovely times there and at home in D'Escousse. Sound good? Yours in Buddha-like serenity and (must be) love, D."

Home in D'Escousse … in a village … in Cape Breton … in the Maritimes … on the edge of the Atlantic. Three light-years from the Pacific – because I've never seen it, don't know what to expect.

Ah come on, cut the drama. You can visit, see a new and beautiful part of the country – nothing hard about that.

But it is hard as hell he's gone now. I am meeting my work commitments, riding Kaber twice a week, walking with Leo, my friends and their dogs. Everything is the same – everything has changed. No matter what happens next, you had enough courage to say *I believe* – I believe love can change us, can make us kinder, can mend tattered hearts and make us softer to the world, but bolder in our passages. It can make us dance.

*One week ago and I am dancing around the pool table at The Reef in Point Roberts. I have my own cue in hand, the one my brother gave me. Plays a charm, and I love to shoot pool. Don is chalking his cue but his eyes are on me. A Fleetwood Mac song from the '70s – "Don't Stop Thinking About Tomorrow" – is blaring from speakers in the corners of the room and I am warbling a harmony. Suddenly Don puts down his cue on the felted pool table and walks to me – eyes filled with stories and feeling. "Are you okay – ?" We hug, and I pull back to look at him again.*

*"Better than that," he says. "For the first time since April, I've remembered what happy is."*

Yesterday's gone, yesterday's gone.

## 13

# MY FIRST TRIP TO THE MARITIMES

*D'ESCOUSSE, CAPE BRETON, OCTOBER 1996*

"I wouldn't be you for all the rice in China!" laughs one of Don's friends, a woman for whom the word petite is too bulky to be of any use as a descriptor. Four-foot-eleven-inch, one-hundred-pound Denise Saulnier is seated at the kitchen table in Don's Cape Breton home, along with her partner Greg and a lot of other people whose names I can't remember. The statement is directed at me – and she isn't the only person at the party to find it amusing. Don was just out of earshot for it and carries on his separate conversation with one of Lulu's brothers – of which there are an astonishing seven in existence, along with two sisters. Three brothers are in attendance this evening.

I have already been checked out by Mrs. Terrio, a woman even tinier than Denise. We weren't in the village more than a few hours before "Mimi" came by to ask me to accompany her on a walk. It wasn't a query; more of a polite command. I stopped my supper preparations, grabbed my coat and did my best to keep up to Mimi's pace as we charged up the hill out of the centre of the village of D'Escousse, where Don has lived since 1971. Mimi dictated the pace of the walk and then direction of the conversation, when we came to be seated on a bench at the top of the hill. She asked me a few questions about what I did for a living, and how Don and I had met.

Niceties aside, she got to the literal heart of the matter. Did I understand that this "noble" man was exhausted and heartbroken? Subtext: Were my intentions honourable? Did I know how hard a battle Lulu had fought against the breast cancer, and how no one really expected to lose her, most of all Don? Subtext: He's still heartbroken, not ready for love. Had I met Lulu's son Mark yet – the son Don had legally adopted when they married seventeen years ago? Subtext: Did I understand how hard it was for him, to have lost his adoring mother and for his father to be seeing someone new, only six months later?

I said yes many times. Yes, Mrs. Terrio, I do know and understand these things to the best of my ability, and according to the short time I've known him. Mimi did not seem completely reassured, but she did seem relieved. She'd "done her part," as a British-born war bride would, no hesitating or beating around the bush. With Lulu gone, her mother was understandably protective of her son-in-law and grandson. Strange women, who dropped out of strange western skies onto Terrio territory, needed to be told their presence was … noted.

*Lulu* – Marie Louise Terrio-Cameron, forty-six years old when she died. Ten years older than me. I can't count how many times I've heard her name spoken this visit, or how many stories about her people have told me, Don most of all. It is as though they and he are compelled to tell me, want to see me nod with great animation, entreat them to tell *just one more*. All of this gives them another chance to breathe her name, to bring to auditory life one who can't be summoned to sight. They love the stories, loved the woman, want to share details of that life and love. It's overwhelming, exhausting – and understandable. There are days I actually feel guilty she died. Or guilty, rather, that I am here and she is not. Other days I just wish I could have one piece of Don that didn't belong heart and soul to Lulu. Maybe I will, maybe I won't. Time will tell.

*Lulu's shadow is long. I hope it won't darken my life.*

I wish I'd had an advocate of my own the day Mimi took me for a walk and a talk. Ha, maybe she'll take me on, if we end up friends. No, impossible, on both counts. About as likely as being true friends with Denise Saulnier. I really like her – love her quick wit and rapid-fire mind – but she was one of Lulu's good friends. I wouldn't blame her if she never felt truly comfortable around me. Too bad. I'd love to learn more about Acadians, too. Maybe she can tell me a bit about that, anyway.

*Were my intentions honourable?* Jesus wept, as my dad would say.

Mimi is only one of seemingly countless people who want to protect Donny, Don, Silver Don, Silver Donald Cameron and Mr. Cameron. The large Terrio family and their families, other friends and neighbours on Isle Madame and around Cape Breton, Maritimers at large, Atlantic Canadians at larger, other Canadians, readers of his books – so many people know about the loss of Lulu and express their sympathy and concern. This isn't even counting his West Coast friends and his own big Cameron family, spread across the country, many of whom call him Donald. I've met his friendly youngest brother, Ken, but that's all. He was warm and watchful. Which is what you'd want to see a sibling be, when a newcomer edges nearer the family campfire.

Doesn't anyone want to protect me? Not on this turf, anyway.

"I wouldn't be you for all the rice in China," says Denise again, thinking I hadn't heard. "Do you understand?" She swirls a hand out in front of her, indicating the assembly and quite possibly the larger world, for all I know.

Yes, I understand. I have to deal with all these people and more. Some I'll have to reassure about my *honourable intentions.* Isn't this a little backwards?

I can't do this. Too many judging and curious eyes. And too many Terrios. If we start in earnest, Don and I, it will be on my home ground again. There, Don only has to deal with my small family – and only occasionally. My friends, too, but they are excited, can't wait to meet him. I don't know when he'll meet Dad, my stepmother Karin and my little sisters Jessica and Fiona, in Ontario. Maybe on a layover, on one of the trips out west.

All in good time. And if it is to be.

# 14

## EARLY DAYS TOGETHER

*FEBRUARY 3, 2011, HALIFAX, NOVA SCOTIA*

We've been so lucky, Don and I, to have lived in so many special places over the years: on the East Coast, Isle Madame, and in Halifax; on the West Coast, Gibson's Landing, Point Roberts, in Washington State, Richmond and Steveston.

We started out living together for the very first time in Gibson's Landing, British Columbia, just north of Vancouver on the Sunshine Coast. Like Point Roberts, Gibson's Landing was another childhood haunt for Don. He loved its immense Douglas firs, long pebbled beaches and quaint, original town centre on the waterfront, near the ferry terminal to the city. I'd spent time in Sechelt, further north, and in Pender Harbour and Powell River, further north again, but had only ever passed through Gibson's, not stayed. In the spring of 1997, Don and I had two odd and lovely months there, renting the home of a speechwriter friend of mine.

Odd: Don's mourning of Lulu was intense and debilitating. Some days he'd get up mid-morning, have coffee and cereal and return to bed to sleep again. The Whippet – for so he was often called, with deep affection – would rise with us and then return to bed with Don. Sometimes I did the same; sometimes I had article deadlines to meet and would go to my computer. Other days I drove to Vancouver for a day of copy-editing at one of several magazines I worked for. Don had quit his position as dean at the University of Cape Breton College at the end of 1996; he, too, worked at assorted freelance jobs, but wasn't taking on much at that time. In addition to a heavy heart, Don was also recovering from a long bout with Graves' Disease. He and Lulu had been ill at the same time, which had made their lives a double nightmare.

Our days were mostly our own that spring. Don's nineteen-year-old son Mark was living in Alberta, working intermittently in the oil patch like so many other displaced "Caper" kids. In retrospect, I understand how upset Mark was with his dad for starting a relationship with me so soon after his mother's death. Teenage Mark was unhappy even before he lost his mother to cancer and her loss took him years to overcome. In those first few years afterwards, he needed more of his father's time than he got – without a stranger in their midst. It just didn't work out that way.

I hope Mark knows how grateful his dad was and is, for Mark's support and love in the first days and weeks after Lulu's passing. Don loved this period of intense closeness between them; he still talks about it. Like most young people, Mark took some years to settle down and find himself, which he has done wonderfully well now, in a secure career and married to a beautiful and warm-hearted Alberta woman, Adriane, known as Andi. Happiness breeds happiness. We all enjoy our time together now.

To me, when I appeared on the Cape Breton scene for my first visit eight months after the loss of his mother, Mark was pleasant and open – astonishingly so, I thought, and had the wit to tell him at the time and later. He may not have wanted me in their lives, but he was never unkind to me.

All the same, that first spring living together with Don, teenage boys were not on my immediate list of preoccupations. There on the West Coast I had more than enough to cope with – Don's fragile emotional and physical health; keeping steady with all my freelance jobs, most of which took a ferry ride to get to; reassuring my family and friends that all was well, despite our relative isolation and almost complete isolation from them; tending my own healing heart;

and growing into a new romantic relationship, unlike any I'd had before.

Lovely: that tropical wave kept curling, tumbling us in the warmest of waters, over and over like tiny sea creatures, weightless, eyes looking up through filtered layers of lemon and aqua. We made love constantly, ate whatever pleased us, took turns curling around a compliant, soft-coated whippet, went on daily walks in the emerald rainforest, beachcombed, played pool at the local pub, hiked the Skookumchuk Trail to the Reversing Rapids, found East Coast patriots in the tiny town of Egmont and snuggled by the woodstove in the evenings, drinking wine and talking about the brilliant and the banal, never sated in our subject range.

We also laughed – more than even we noticed.

"So tell me," asked my oldest sister Zoë, a month into my Gibson's sojourn with Don, "are you enjoying living with Don?" Zoë was ringing me from Courtenay, on Vancouver Island, where she lived with her husband Garney and daughter Jocelyn. I'd been writing regular letters to our dad, as always, but hadn't been as good with my siblings. She was dead curious for news.

"Zoë," I said, voice pitched low because Don was napping, "we are having so much fun. He thinks I am the funniest woman alive –"

"– because you are," she interrupted, laughing herself.

"– and we laugh our fool heads off at almost everything we say. Goofy idiots, really, but who cares? It suits us."

"So all this is working out well – I don't have to worry about you?" Geoffrey said the same thing last week. In this part of the country, there are people who worry about *me* – it's kind of nice. Nice to have older siblings, who pleasantly fuss about my welfare. I do the same with them, so it evens out. We are, understandably, a worry-prone family.

"Well," I said, "there is one thing that isn't quite right." It's actually been bothering me right now, as we've been talking and laughing. "It's my stomach – there's something quite weird going on. My guts just ache, like too many sit-ups or someone's punched me – honestly, it hurts like hell, I can't imagine what –"

"Marjorie! I think I know what's wrong!" She was laughing in that childlike, uncontrollable way she has sometimes, a way that slays me with affection.

"Ow," I said, mid-laugh. "This is exactly what I am talking about, my guts really hur –"

"It's from laughing!" she howls. "You've actually pulled a gut from laughing." She was right – I had.

Later that day, Zoë related this conversation to her daughter Jocelyn, age twelve. "Mum," said Jocelyn, "Marjorie is going to marry that man, I just know it."

## 15

## MY FIRST SUMMER IN THE MARITIMES

*FEBRUARY 9, 2011, HALIFAX, NOVA SCOTIA*

The summer of 1997 was spectacular. Day after day of sun, warm and occasionally hot temperatures, a little rain overnight and clear skies by dawn.

"Are the Maritimes always like this?" I asked, wide-eyed, ready to believe. Some things don't change.

"Oh yes," said Don. "Every year." He smiled. Then elaborately winked.

We sailed locally in Lennox Passage and a little further from home, in the Bras d'Or Lakes. We sailed on our own – Don, Leo and I – and "in company," with Denise Saulnier and Greg Silver, who sailed their catboat, *Queen Celeste*. Greg and Denise had moved from Halifax to D'Escousse in 1996, though they'd known Don and Lulu, initially in a business context, for ten years before that.

Against the odds, my friendship with Denise had taken off like a polo pony nicked by a spur. I loved her brilliant mind and darting sense of humour. A graphic designer by trade and an amateur historian by interest, she also *knew stuff* – on the broadest scale of anyone I'd ever known, aside from Don. If we went to a country auction, Denise knew about what we were looking at, knew how much we should bid on an item or when we shouldn't bother. From her and other Acadians, I learned about the Acadian people and their history, a subject I knew nil about before moving to Cape Breton. It was all so fresh and fascinating to me, especially when she told stories *de sa famille and les autres familles de la région de Clare*, which she did so entertainingly and with great affection.

I'd always had and have brainy friends. But Acadienne Denise was so entirely different from anyone I knew on the West Coast. She was an original.

Greg and Denise ran a graphic design company. Like Don and I, they worked from home, which was a short walk up the road from our house. Once the four of us began to spend time together, we were almost completely content in each other's company. My jealous, cavewoman's heart stopped wondering if Lulu and Don had had more fun with Greg and Denise than we did – and simply counted my blessings they were in my life. My transition to country life would have been so much harder without their accepting, loving hearts – maybe even impossible. There were days the four of us together was like a perfect little symphony of laughter and sharing.

I managed to ride just once that summer, with a young neighbour who had horses, but mostly it was a boat year, as was the following summer.

Other than a brief summer sailing course as a teenager, the first boat experiences I'd ever had were on commercial vessels – trollers, to be exact. The artisans of the fleet, they are called, because they catch what they intend to catch, one tidy and lethal hook after another. By-catch is negligible. So I still loved the sound of big commercial diesel engines and thought boat time mostly meant getting from A to B in a timely manner. One was supposed to make money, after all.

Sailing was all about silent passage over the water – maybe some *jekoosh, jekoosh* against the hull – at whichever speed the wind dictated. Slowly but surely I was getting used to "the flappy things" – jumbo, main, jib, fisherman, mule, spinnaker, all sorts of names to memorize – but I couldn't comprehend the choice of no engine. Don was proud *Silversark* didn't have an engine. You have to be a damn good sailor to sail without one. But even good sailors can be stuck a quarter mile from a wharf – for hours – on a windless day.

I was not fit company the day this happened to us, just outside of St. Peter's. Out on the water we stayed, out on deck we stayed – no wheelhouse on *Silversark* – the rain steady on our heads, a thunder and lightning storm in full swing all around us. Our only movement was lateral as we tacked back and forth, back and forth, across the narrow, sandy channel. Don remained cheerful, a sign of good things to come.

But an engine in *Silversark* ("Silver's Ark") was several years off, as was a new motor-sailer boat, *Magnus*, which would take us on to far-off adventures in tropical waters. For those first two summers sailing together, we stayed on home turf for Don and new turf (surf, actually) for me. One frustrating day aside, I was a contented new sailor, dazzled at the beauty of the Bras d'Or Lakes, an inland sea, I learned. Black-back gulls, petrels, bald eagles, herons – I loved seeing all the different birds wheel, dart and plummet and grew to appreciate the quiet that permitted me to hear them, too. The lake waters were silky and warm for swimming and *Silversark* is a cosy, beautifully finished boat. It doesn't have standing headroom, as the design was intended for offshore sailing. It does have a wide and comfortable V-berth, an inviting galley table and a well-designed, workable galley.

I was in the galley one early evening that first summer in D'Escousse. We were at anchor in a green and gold cove, just Don, Leo and me. My shoulders were hunched down and my head was lowered; even at five feet two inches, I couldn't stand upright either. I might have been peeling a potato. More likely, it being a warm summer evening, I was making a salad. I was preparing a meal of some sort. Yes, there was a glass of wine nearby – but no, I hadn't had much to drink. It was one of those rare moments of complete contentment that come to a life. If I was slicing a tomato or a bunch of green onions, then I could have done that forever. The air was soft and the cabin had its own indefinable smell – a mix, maybe, of suntan lotion, salt air and water, warmed teak and a lavender hand-soap by the sink. No music on the tape deck, no short-wave radio on for a weather forecast. The boat was dipping and creaking as wooden boats do, but so gently and only now and then. My feet were bare, spread apart for balance on the wooden sole. My face was warm and rosy from a day in the sun. I rarely feel pretty, but I was pretty in that moment, even beautiful. Looking into the small mirror above the sink I saw sun-bleached hair, jade-blue eyes and a mouth that had been kissed into puffiness.

I heard my mum's voice, the day I came home from that first visit with Don in Point Roberts: "You've been well-loved," she said smiling, and stroked my hair tenderly – *oh, how Barbara, my mother, had loved Richard, my father, and cherished her time with him*. I dipped my head in embarrassment at my mother's words, but did not deny them. I smiled, thinking about the memory – and then felt a kiss on my cheek. Like a bird feather just touching the skin. My hand went to my cheek, which tingled.

"Don?" He was nowhere to be seen. I heard a series of creaks. He was still on deck, from the sounds of it coming back to the cockpit from the bow.

"Don?" I asked again, softer this time, knowing he had nothing to do with this kiss. My hand was still on my cheek. "That you?"

It wasn't Don. It wasn't Mum, either. I've always known it was Lulu, saying goodbye to her guy and their boat – and saying hello to me. I think my feet were planted right where hers had been, so many times; it was just so easy for her to touch me. I also think it was her way of saying thank you. Everyone had been so worried about Don after he lost Lulu. Mark thought he was going to lose both parents, Don in short order after his mother. The kiss said, *It's all right now, isn't it? I don't have to worry about him anymore, do I?*

All I could manage was a nod. Then many little nods in succession, seen only by her. My cheek felt different all that evening.

My seventy-three-year-old father had already jokingly given fifty-nine-year-old Don his blessing to marry me. I always figured I'd had a blessing of another sort.

*16*

## GETTING MARRIED

### Wedding Invitation

If I gave you my ocean ...
... *I'd give you mine.*
Along with my love
*Returned in kind.*
Then we should marry.
*Splendid notion!*
You and me *and a world of oceans.*

Marjorie Lorraine Simmins and Silver Donald Cameron invite you to join them on the occasion of their wedding on Saturday, March 14, 1998 at 11:30 a.m., at the Unitarian Church 949 West 49th Avenue, Vancouver, B.C. A lunch reception in the adjacent church hall will follow the ceremony. A Cape Breton kitchen racket will follow this summer.

R.S.V.P. Mrs. Barbara Simmins

Chaplain Geoffrey Simmins:

"Donald and Marjorie, I invite you now to join hands as you repeat your vows. The hand offered by each of you is an extension of self, just as is your mutual love. Cherish the touch, for you touch not only your own but also another life. Be sensitive to its pulse. Seek always to understand and respect its rhythm.

"Please repeat after me, your vows:

"In the presence of this company, I, Donald, take you, Marjorie, to be my wife,

"In the presence of this company, I, Marjorie, take you, Donald, to be my husband,

"to have and to hold,

"from this day forward,

"and forsaking all others,

"for better, for worse,

"for richer, for poorer,

"in sickness and in health,

"in sorrow and in joy,

"in reflection and in laughter,

"to work and to share,

"to grow and adventure,

"to love and to cherish,

"for as long as we both shall live.

"Donald/Marjorie, repeat after me: With this ring I wed you, with my body I honour you, with my soul I sing with you, through all the days of our lives.

"Now you will feel no rain, for each of you will be shelter for the other,

"Now you will feel no cold, for each of you will be warmth for the other,

"Now you are two persons, but there is only one life before you."

Wedding Poem for Marjorie & Don
by Zoë Landale

Walking down to Heart's Desire beach in the afternoon
you think about iris, the blue of them deep
enough to catch the heart. Fleur-de-lis
of petals, heraldic in a wedding bouquet.

The beach is on two coasts. It has many names.
Fraser River with its glide of tugs and chip barges, outrageously blue
water piled by summer westerly into peaks;
broom, gold and vital, blooming all along the wild lands.

Pondville with its clean fine sand, almost tropical,
the Labrador current sliding gelid offshore. The saltmarsh
where once in winter a brown muskrat furiously swam
beneath a quarter inch of glass.

Whatever shore you take the dog to,
he finds a stick way too big for him and picks it up.
This is the locus of the world, one fawn and white whippet
trotting, a silver log in his mouth.

Walking down to Heart's Desire beach in the afternoon
you clatter with shells of words
left over from the day's work.
You are glad of a companion

who understands the way words curve
and rattle, translucent with a mother-of-pearl gleam.
A companion who makes you laugh so hard
your stomach gets sore.

A person who understands the value of candles,
how during the dark hours
your house must be sprinkled with star points,
the flames blessing every corner with flicker and glow.

Walking down to Heart's Desire beach in the afternoon
you have lots of time to think about dinner.
The greenness of broccoli, how oranges are punctuation,
periods magnified; the tang of them in salad.

There are many things you are grateful for:
the moment last summer between beaches,
sailboat slicing along in silence,
where you were so happy you could hardly speak.

When you come in the door now, you can call out
*Hello! I'm home,*
and there will be an answer.
Always an answer.

And the smell of curries, roast chicken,
vinaigrettes, lemon meringue pie
and chocolate chip cookies
are home, and a hand that reaches out in warmth

is home, and you are always home now
no matter what coast you are on
the blue of water reminding you of iris
and the words that bind you two

*For better for worse, for richer for poorer*
*in sickness and in health for as long as we both shall live:*
these are flames you take with you in daylight
walking down to Heart's Desire beach in the afternoon.

## FEBRUARY 8, 2011, HALIFAX, NOVA SCOTIA

I wouldn't be the first or last bride to say it, but truly, our wedding day was perfect. Rainy Vancouver? Not that day. The sun was full-on and the Japanese cherry, azaleas and forsythia were in early, vigorous bloom in the church gardens and courtyard. A friendly neighbour kitty was the first guest to arrive in the church – a blessing from the animal world, in my view. She was ushered out only because of the numerous canine guests who would assemble in the courtyard later on.

The church pianist, as requested, played Handel – Water Music, of course, for the aqua wave that curled and tumbled onto two coasts now. Family and friends joined us from across the country. Don's oldest friend from high school and his wife drove up from California, with a box of wine as a much-enjoyed wedding gift. A beloved friend of Don's, the brilliant Paul Fougère, had flown in from Halifax to do our flowers – the church and table arrangements, a bouquet, the boutonnières and corsages – and make the gorgeous cake. "What a generous man," said my father, when he learned of Paul's contributions to our wedding. "Could you buy him a drink from me?"

A professional stylist, Paul also arranged my hair, cut Don's hair – and coloured Mark's hair, which was, when he arrived in from Alberta, a vivid shade of orange. By the time Paul had Mark spruced up, people asked if he'd given up on the oil patch and started modelling.

Tall, dark-haired, with bright hazel eyes, Mark was our handsome best man. Beside him stood Don's younger brother David. Brother Ken, the youngest Cameron brother, would be the reception MC. Standing with me were my oldest sister Zoë and her daughter Jocelyn. Don and Jocelyn have been fast friends since the day they met. Once they became friends, the time before that seemed indistinct, hard to remember. I knew something about that.

The Unitarian Church was a big part of our lives in those days. My mother not only attended services each Sunday but worked throughout the year with a team of other senior women on the monster once-a-year thrift sale. The event was popular with Vancouverites and a big money-maker for the church. I'd been to the thrift sale many times and had even helped Mum out a very small bit one year. I was thus comfortable in this particular sacred space, which is modern and airy, with adjoining buildings that are lower scale and equally pleasant. There is an Asian sensibility to the overall design of the church, courtyard and gardens.

My brother Geoffrey, an architectural historian who teaches at the University of Calgary, is also a deeply spiritual man; at the time of our wedding, he had just become a Unitarian chaplain. With the ink still drying on his chaplain's papers, he was just able to perform the wedding ceremony for Don and me. I have rarely been happier in this life than looking up at the brother I love to bits to hear the vows I was to repeat, and then looking at the man I love to bits to repeat those vows. I was so glad I wasn't married by a stranger. Besides, if your big brother tells you to do something – pay attention, it's serious! None of this stopped me from beaming throughout the ceremony, buoyed beyond description by the rightness and brightness of the moment. Nor from laughing outright when I kissed Don – and discovered *by jeez*, he'd been into the rum already. Dutch courage has its uses!

After the ceremony we gathered in the courtyard for people hugs, dog hugs, chatter and photos. Leo wore a collar of flowers and knew, somehow, he was Top Dog that day. The other dogs belonged to my girlfriends, almost all of whom have one or more each. I loved hearing the barks and yips of all the special dogs in our lives and I love having wedding photos with English pointers, a pug, two whippets, a Schipperke and a golden Labrador retriever.

Our wedding photos show pink and gold floral profusions as background, and a bare-armed bride. It wasn't actually warm enough for that bit of bravado, but my dress was sleeveless and I only wore the short cape I bought to go with it before the ceremony, not afterwards. My ever-generous mother paid for the elegant Jessica McClintock dress and cape. We picked them out together, at a small and romantic wedding-dress store on 10th Avenue near Sasamat. I surprised myself by choosing a traditional dress. One look at the white on white floral pattern, the fitted bodice and flowing skirt and I was pretty sure all the other practical choices were no longer in the running. When Mum gasped when I stepped out of the change room in it, I knew for certain.

The reception was held in the church hall. The smoked salmon lasagna was divine, as were the numerous salads, breads and wedding cake. There were the usual and some unusual toasts. Don's beloved eighty-five-year-old Aunt Ethel gave a splendid one to the groom and my brother-in-law Garney, Zoë's husband, did a fine and funny job talking about me. I toasted the entire gathering. When I began my speech to acknowledge my mother, family and friends, I wasn't sure if I could keep speaking. I paused for the longest time – nor would I look up from the page in my hand – and then I carried on. When I finally did look up, I saw every one of my girlfriends crying and Mum "destroyed," as a Brit would say. Good thing I didn't look up! Twelve-year-old Jocelyn performed "The Toast to Absent Friends" from *The Wind in the Willows* and did a brilliant job of it. We were all convinced she'd go on to have a career in the theatre. I was in awe, actually, that such a young girl could do such a clever thing. Don flat-out loved the performance and was the first to shoot to his feet to start the clapping when she finished.

My little sisters Jessica and Fiona flew in from Ottawa to be with us, though Dad's health was getting fragile and he chose not to come along. My stepmother Karin thought my mum would be uncomfortable with her presence and also did not attend.

By 4:00 we were on our own and drove down to Granville Island. We had changed into casual but dressy clothes and at 5:00 boarded a boat for a supper cruise around Vancouver Harbour and Burrard Inlet. Beyond several bites of lunch and a sip or two of wine – I was so elevated emotionally, I feared I would trip and fall if I drank at all; food was similarly impossible to ingest – I hadn't eaten all day. We fell upon the buffet and bottle of rich red wine. At 9:00 we disembarked and drove to another one of our heart's homes, the house we rented in Point Roberts, Washington, for three springs in a row. That year, I called it the "honeymoon cottage." The day after the wedding it would be the site of a rocking party, with almost everyone from the previous day in attendance. We even had our own Cape Breton fiddler, Greg Silver, who had flown out from D'Escousse. Denise, to my extreme sadness, was unable to come to the wedding.

The morning after the party, a letter from my Aunt Susette in York, England, arrived at the post office. Susette was my father's only sister. She was a psychiatric nurse by profession, a hedonist and enthusiast by nature, and a creative, brainy and affectionate woman. Although her childhood was gothic in its torments, we young Simmins often called Susette the "sanest Simmins in generations." She loved well and she lived well.

## MARCH 1998

*My very dear Marjorie and Don*

*So many good, warm and positive thoughts do I send to you both. Somehow I don't feel that I've left any of the fairy godmothers out – not even the awfully earnest ones. I lay in bed this morning thinking of all the gifts that marriage bestows – love, laughter, understanding, peace, freedom to be, the ability to see beyond that which is ordinary in each other; oh on and on it went.*

*We human beings are an interesting lot, and we are so wonderfully different from all the other animals, and so much more exciting. You two, in choosing each other, have already opened so many new doors, explored new lanes and listened to each other. And the lovely thing is that these things will never stop. I and my partner Beryl have been together for 40 years, and every single day there is something new to see, and new roads to walk down which didn't seem to be there yesterday. I wish for you what I have had for myself, that inexpressible joy of complete togetherness.*

*I wish I had been able to find you wedding presents. Being an English medieval city, York doesn't cater to the esoteric. I'm sorry it's money – but the best I can do.*

*God bless you both and I love you.*
*Susette*

"It is quite possible for us to have thirty years together," I said to Don, passing him the letter. "Forty might be stretching it." I giggled, the idea of a 101-year-old Don and a 79-year-old Marjorie not having much appeal to a "young" bride of thirty-nine. And good lord, The Whippet would be forty-five!

"Thirty sounds fine," he smiled, "but only if we do it as well as Susette and Beryl."

"I wish they could marry."

"You never know. There may come a time when British law will permit them to."

"Hard to imagine. But wouldn't it be great?"

(In 2004, civil unions became legal in Britain for gay and lesbian partners. Susette and Beryl married that year. Susette's Canadian family sent flowers and champagne to the reception. We were thrilled. Susette, bless her, was overwhelmed with joy, as was Beryl. We lost our Susette in 2007. But we still have her words, and her great faith in enduring love. We continue to write letters to Beryl.)

## 17

# SETTLING INTO MY MARITIME LIFE

*FEBRUARY 9, 2011, HALIFAX, NOVA SCOTIA*

If I needed a reminder I hadn't married an invisible Mr. Smith, it came in the form of an article in *Frank Magazine*, the Atlantic issue, July 14, 1998. I was also reminded that Lulu would always be a part of my life, not just Don's – and that I was a first-time-married but *third* wife. We had been home from B.C. since May and had had our "kitchen racket party" – for two hundred people – the first week of July.

SILVER DONALD TAKES ANOTHER WIFE; CONFIDENT AUTHOR PASSES ON VIAGRA, blared one of its headlines on the cover page. Inside the article, the "journalist" had much to say:

"This past Saturday was a big day in D'Escousse: friends of Silver Donald Cameron gathered at his home for a party to meet his new wife. The noted author was married out West to Marjorie Simmins, a BC magazine writer, in March. Marjorie is 39; Silver Don, also known as an avid sailor and unofficial ambassador for the Bras d'Or Lakes, is a remarkable 61 (and certainly doesn't need any Viagra yet – ed.)

"He and Marjorie met several years ago when she interviewed him about one of his books. They hooked up again a year ago. She was a house guest at his home in the fishing village of D'Escousse last summer and has already proved her own writing credentials locally by penning pieces for The Herald (an outsider's experience at a Cape Breton bingo hall, etc., etc.).

"Silver Donald and Marjorie plan to winter on the West Coast and summer in Cape Breton. The author first discovered Isle Madame during the fisheries strike in the early 70s and purchased his home at D'Escousse in 1982 ...

"When he arrived in the 70s, the BC native had just finished prof'ing duties at the UNB. He arrived initially with his first wife, Ann Cameron.

"The author's second wife, Lulu, was the daughter of Mimi and the late Arthur Terrio, D'Escousse natives. While Silver Donald and Lulu had no children of their own, she had a son, Mark ... [from an earlier marriage]. Mark, 20, is currently in Red Deer. [Don legally adopted Mark at the time of his marriage to Lulu.]

"Although Lulu was given a Catholic send-off from St. Hyacinth's RC church, I understand it was pretty much by invitation only. One resident compared the service to the one that lamented Princess Diana, given the tributes and speeches she received.

"Silver Donald said his wedding was attended by writers, editors and other literati. His friends on this coast include such literary luminaries as Farley Mowat, who summers near St. Peter's and Parker Barss Donham, the Laird of Boularderie.

" ... he hopes to get his 27-foot sailboat back in ship-shape soon and resume his voyages this season.

"Silver Don's new book – his 15th – is The Living Beach (MacMillan Canada)."

They'd noticed the bingo essay, I'd noted with relief. That was good. I didn't want to slack off with the writing; I'd worked too long and too hard for that. I wasn't Marjorie Cameron – unless it made a little old village lady happy to call me so. Then it was lovely, an honour. But in regular life, I was Marjorie Simmins, freelance writer and journalist. It was enough of a challenge to take on a new homeland. I was determined not to lose my voice – and who I was at a cellular level – in the process.

The *Frank Magazine* article didn't perturb either of us. It only made us laugh. The rag is silly and often inaccurate in its reportings – but it is widely read. I did feel a bit exposed.

Ah well, I was grateful they'd spelled my unusual surname name right; that was thanks to Don actually taking the call from the reporter, to make sure they got some facts correct, unlike their usual botch jobs at *Frank*. Even the teasing parts of the "article" were all right. I told Don that it did his reputation no harm to have fictitiously declined Viagra.

What did perturb me, earlier on and throughout that year, was Don's insistence that he was going to write a book about Lulu. It would focus on their lives together, he said – but mostly her life, the one that was so unfairly cut short. There needed to be a record, he continued, of all her high-spirited adventures, all the odds she had beaten – if not the last, mortal one – to live the very finest sort of life, full of challenge and satisfaction. He would mention the book idea every few months. He mentioned it before we married, he elaborated on it after we married.

I was shocked at how resistant I felt about Don writing the book. Selfishly, I knew it would mean that I would live more closely with Lulu than I even had already and continued to do. Don's grief about Lulu's loss was never far away. I wanted to see him heal more, not think about every sad event of the two-year battle against cancer that she'd lost. That *they'd* lost. I knew that.

But I was a newlywed. I wanted to keep my happiness all to myself.

I started to wonder about the kiss on the boat. *Sometimes things are not as they seem.*

We both kept writing. It was a time of discovery and learning. Most of all, as Susette had hoped for us, it was a time of "inexpressible joy of complete togetherness." I actually felt I had two lovers, Don and Cape Breton, both vying for the lion's share of my affections. Added to this happiness was the emotional security I derived from our West Coast springtime sojourns, five years running. The Pacific-coast world, I was relieved to see, wasn't going anywhere in my absence. I settled into my Maritime life, all eyes and ears.

## BINGO NIGHT
### D'ESCOUSSE, NOVA SCOTIA, 1998

"What colour dabber do you want?" asks the woman working the cash register adjacent the inner doors of the community hall. She steps sideways to reveal the shelf behind her, with its tidy rows of coloured markers. Green, purple, red, blue, they're all nice rich colours. Then I see a particular favourite.

"Hot pink, please." She is halfway to the shelf when another voice halts her progress.

"Not pink. She'll take a red one, please." Surprised, I turn to my new friend, from whom the correction has come. What's the matter with … ?

"Pink is two dollars," she explains, "red is only one."

Oh, I see. Sort of. Saving money I understand, but for some mysterious reason, pink ink is more expensive than the other coloured inks. Drat, we're not even in the hall yet, and already my ignorance is showing.

It's funny, but I feel as though I should know how to do this, if only by virtue of birthplace. I am, as my father has told me often and with pride, a seventh-generation Canadian. (No matter that he added his family's time in Canada together with my mother's family's time here, for that sum.) And yet, at thirty-eight years old, I have missed out on a quintessential Canadian experience: BINGO. Tapping my fingers on the counter I wait for the cashier to give me change from my twenty-dollar bill, borrowed earlier in the day from a neighbour. Change received, I move aside for the next person in line to buy a dabber.

As I wait I scan the crowd around us and see the familiar face of a woman who owns a local store. I call hello and wave. The response is immediate, unprefaced by any sort of greeting.

"You're a bingo player?" Her tone is both shocked and pleased. I pause for just a moment, trying to interpret the voice shadings. Maybe she figures people from the West Coast have never even heard of the game. Maybe she's just glad to see me out at a community event. Either way, she's smiling bright as a Cape Breton hillside in the autumn.

"You bet I am, first time, too," I answer.

The right answer apparently, as it's greeted by a loud whoop of laughter.

"First time lucky, you'll see," she says. "Have fun."

Her prediction triggers a belated and startling thought: my odds for winning are as good as anyone else's here. Who knows, I could be returning that borrowed twenty by night's end, peeled from a nice plump wad in my jeans pocket.

Markers in hand, my friend and I enter the stadium-sized hall. As my friend had warned me, the air is a theatre curtain of cigarette smoke. As I'd told her, it doesn't bother me, because I smoke, too.

We work our way down a long row of tables, buying a sheet of numbers from the volunteers sitting at each one. A loonie here, a toonie there, by the end of the row I've spent $10 and have 18 playing sheets; from the front door to here, that's a $13 lay out.

More than a video, less than a night at the movies.

Not that there's a movie theatre around here. Yet another reason I'm in the hall tonight. When in Rome – or in this case, the village of D'Escousse on Isle Madame, Nova Scotia – enjoy local offerings. I may be a city girl from far-off Vancouver, but I know enough to lay the turf green side up.

Through the crowded room we weave, finding a table to sit at on the perimeter of the room. There are no open doors and the air is thick and hot. It's loud too, with near to five hundred people gathered for the evening's activities. I glance at my watch. Ten minutes to go. Slowly the conversation begins to dwindle: the atmosphere feels pre-Indy, all eyes waiting for a checkered flag to drop.

Except there are no flags, only welcoming words from the night's host, his voice magnified by a microphone. I turn in my chair to see where he is seated. There he is behind us, stationed high above the crowd at a table on the stage. The Keeper of Numbers. The Bestower of Luck. Looks young enough, but if he's like everyone else around here, he's probably been a bingo buff since … what's that expression I heard last week?

Oh yeah, since Christ wore gumboots.

And God indeed, if my family heard me say that, they'd collapse laughing. She's gone native. No, I haven't. Couldn't, if I tried for the rest of my days. May as well have "from away," another local expression, tattooed on my forehead. Which doesn't mean I haven't been welcomed on the East Coast, or that I can't enjoy – and use, with my give-away bland accent – the original turns of phrase that swirl around me.

D'Escousse is home, after all, for six months of this year, and will be, for many half-years to come. I'd like to fit in, as best I can. And fully enjoy myself along the way.

"Ready to play?"

I nod briskly at my friend, then realize that no, I'm not ready. I don't even know which page we're playing first – and what's everyone doing with their markers?

"Give me your sheets," says my friend. "I'll put them in order."

Swish, swish, swish, the job's done. "Now shake your marker, then dab it, like this." Thump, thump, thump, the tip of her marker meets paper, and is now primed and ready to go. I copy her motions precisely, and childlike, am tempted to ask for praise when fat, ink-soaked circles appear on the thin paper. Fortunately, there's no opportunity, as my friend is already explaining something else.

"The centre squares are free."

She points to and then quickly marks the blank centre squares inside each of the six larger box shapes on my first sheet of paper. This seems straightforward enough until I glance around me at the other players' sheets: why do theirs all have nine boxes and mine only has six?

"G 60," says the host.

Okay, the question will have to come later. Along with solving the mystery of over-priced pink markers. Time to pay attention: B, I, N, G – stop, down, no G 60s. In any of the six boxes. Not a propitious beginning.

"N 34." Got it, in three boxes.

My friend reaches over and dabs two squares on my sheet with her blue marker.

"B 5," she says, "there and there."

B 5? When did the host say that?

"Watch the screen," she explains, pointing to the wall ahead of us. Sure enough, there's a big TV screen that shows the balls before the host reads the numbers on them. A second television is set up behind us. Dab, pause, dab. At least I no longer need my friend's help. And next time, I'll be fast enough to monitor a sheet with nine boxes.

But six is fine for now.

A groundswell of sound – not quite conversation, more dense that mumbles – has begun. Must be almost time.

"Bingo!"

For this round, two lines of numbers, in any direction, have been completed. The winner sits not far from us, her hand raised to catch the host's attention. A moment later, the serial number on her sheet has been matched up with the computer's record of its numbers – another screen I hadn't noticed, despite the red neon lights – and her win is confirmed. A volunteer jogs through the crowd to hand over the cash prize.

By the third game I am totally relaxed, even nonchalant in attitude and movement. Eyes, ears and hands work in unison, like driving a car.

"You're marking well," says my friend. Student and teacher beam at one another, well content with progress made.

"And you're set for any two lines, you know that, don't you?"

Set for any two lines? Doesn't that mean ...

"Get ready to call."

I glance up from the last number I need to win to hear that same number called: a moment of hubris and I'd forgotten to watch the screens. Sloppy on the curve of the road, but I'm in the straightaway now.

"BINGO!"

Snap, snap, snap, snap, snap.

Five twenty-dollar bills appear on the table beside my right elbow. And I can't stop laughing, with delight and disbelief. A first-time player, a one in five hundred chance to come up lucky.

"I won! A hundred bucks! Hey, this is the easiest loot I've ever made. What a great game." I leave the bills on the table, admiring the modest-sized green stack for a full minute before folding it away in the pocket of my jeans. At which point, stillness all around me, I manage to remember my manners. But again, I'm slow off the mark. I listen, abashed, as a trio of voices passes by my good intentions.

"A hundred dollars, that's great."

"Good for you."

"Glad you're having fun."

Pleasure mingles with winner-guilt as my friend and the other players at our table generously extend their congratulations. I've no way of knowing for certain, but I'd guess there aren't a lot of spare twenties lining the pockets around me. And I'd feel a bit happier in this winning if they knew the same was actually true for me.

"You know what? I borrowed a twenty to come here tonight. Damn, now I have to return it."

Eight faces crease into easy smiles, and one belly laugh triggers the laughter of all. A real bingo, with my timing right at last.

By night's end my take-home hasn't increased, but I've learned all the different patterns to win: two lines any way, cross and T-shapes, full card and more. I've also learned that the pink ink, unlike the other coloured inks, is fluorescent – apparently more expensive to produce. Along with five hundred other pairs of hands, I've applauded the winning of the $4,000 "Cookie Jar," which, according to the gasps and squeals of the recipient, was sweet indeed. A wonderful evening, but I'm tired now – my eyes especially – and ready to go home. My friend and I exit a side door of the hall and walk together under a richly starred country sky. My home, happily, is minutes away.

"Are you going to play next week?" My friend is an avid player, goes to three games each week. She wasn't a winner tonight, but is obviously pleased that I was, and may even now consider me a full-fledged convert to the game. Once a month anyway. More than that and my eyes will go buggy from the long parade of numbers. But less than that and the odds will keep me a one-hit wonder. Remember the turf, two-coast girl: green side up.

"I'll phone you soon. Count on it."

## HOME PORTS
### D'ESCOUSSE, NOVA SCOTIA, 1998

"Watch the road, you're swerving." At ten at night after a day that began in Ontario and ended in Nova Scotia, I was not, in May of this year, the most cheerful company ever to grace a passenger seat.

"I am not swerving," said the beaming driver. "I'm dancing. A jig. Can't you tell?"

Well, no, can't say I'd figured that one out. Saw dance-like movements – the twist and stretch of shoulders and the rhythmic bounce of a knee – but thought that was more connected to a long day of travel than dancing to a happy CD of the soul. And besides, we weren't actually at the end of our trip yet, so what exactly was it we were celebrating?

"We're on the island!" And this time there was no mistaking his enthusiastic if seat-restricted motions as dance, or his obvious pleasure when we crossed the causeway from Cape Breton to Isle Madame. There is only one island in this world that so captivates this man with whom I share my life. And only one village, towards which we drove that night, that for him meets all the complex needs of mind, heart and spirit. I stifled a weary sigh: it was definitely not the moment to say I missed, already, the sky-sweeping red cedars and Douglas firs of the province I grew up in. Or my family, many of whom were now four thousand miles away. "Nearly home," I managed instead to say brightly. Which in truth did not help matters much, in terms of evoking a less conflicted state of consciousness. In the past two years, since the earliest days of our co-adventuring, the word "home" has become so elastic, I sometimes feel I could claim a new definition for it with each day that passes.

Try as I may, I cannot anymore limit the meaning of home to a single idea, or contain it within a single walled space. In the long term, I know this will be a blessing, to feel loved and welcomed on two coasts, and at various family oases in between. In the short term, I consider the definitions of home as they come to me, testing their firmness like the careful press of a hiker's boot on an unfamiliar path.

And familiarity does seem to be a key to feeling at home. That, and predictability and psychic comfort, within the places we rest at during our annual travels across the country. At my sister's Vancouver Island home, the surrounding garden offers a year-round abundance of flowers and vegetables. Her kitchen presents different fragrances throughout the day: sweet cinnamon in the morning, baking bread by noon and the hunger-producing tang of garlic come evening. My husband and I are welcome, even feted, in the bright interiors of my sister's house. During the day we beachcomb or hike through sun-dappled forest trails, where green is a scent, a texture, a rainbow gradation of light to dark. In the evening, candlelight glows in the living room; we gather around it on soft cushions and store, deep within us, the rhythm and cadence of family voices.

My mother's voice is low-pitched, though it rises with pleasure when we visit her at her suburban Vancouver home. On the kitchen table, a stack of library books waiting to be devoured; in the living room, the coffee table is strewn with magazines and atlases. "One more chapter," her four children would plead with her at bedtime, "read us just one more." And each night, a pause, a smile and the ritual words, "One more" – then all voices chimed together – "and that's absolutely the last." The home of books began early, remains an essential joy for all of us.

The company of my brother is another home, days of then and days of now centred in liking, edged by laughter. In teenage years, out came the playing cards – endless games of speed, crib and poker – and on went the tea kettle – oceans of Earl Grey, poured into thick-lipped Chinatown mugs. Not much conversation as we played, not much required. Stability of presence – warm, accepting – was the need that was met. And is met still, with visits, phone calls and letters.

Letters from my father, too; hundreds in a single year, they detail his busy and creative life in Ottawa. We shared a family home for only eight years. But he has spent the past thirty-one helping me to establish and keep a spiritual home. "God grant me the serenity to accept the things I cannot change, the courage to change the things I can, and the wisdom to know the difference – try to live this, it helps in tough times," my father said time and time again. I tried, and it did, also time and again. I was twenty before I knew the mantra came from Alcoholics Anonymous. At thirty-nine, I still repeat the Serenity Prayer and other AA wisdoms my father has shared with me, whenever times get "tough." His God – who has supported my father's sobriety for over thirty years, and mine – who has aided me whenever called on – appear to live in the same house. But my father gave me the street map to get there.

"Are you missing home?" My husband's voice pulled me back into the present moment, though with so many thoughts layered one on the other, I wasn't quite sure how to answer his question. Still quiet, I reached out a hand to his wrist. Warm skin, steady pulse and the face that smiled at me the light and the laughter of all my days: home each day, every day. A moment later, from behind us in the car, came a tired whimper. I twisted in my seat and placed a hand on top of my dog's silky head. Long walks on the beaches of the Atlantic and Pacific, in the company of the bravest, most generous of canine hearts: the whippet creates home, too.

A mile later, when the tall blue house by the water's edge appeared on our left, my heart said "home" long before hand's touch or body's shelter. In we stepped, to our wonderful, once-upon-a-sea-captain's house in D'Escousse, on Isle Madame. Another place of contentment, this one ringed by silver oaks. These trees sweep the sky, too. Four months away, I had forgotten that. But it takes time for the landscapes of new homes to imprint themselves on memory and to affect the spirit.

It may take time for landscapes to settle beneath the skin, but not seascapes, if you're coastal-raised. When I look out the window of my workroom to Lennox Passage, I do not see the trollers, seiners and gillnetters of the West Coast commercial fishing fleet I know so well. But I do see brightly painted Cape Islanders and the long, low hulls of Northumberland Strait vessels. I like the capable look of these boats, would love to crew aboard them for a day of fishing. Smells of diesel, coffee and fish: working boats are a homescape no matter where I live. I watch their steady progress over choppy waters, and search, on some days, for home port lettering on their sterns.

## COASTAL LIVES
### BOUNDARY BAY, BRITISH COLUMBIA, 2000

Don: The paddles bite the water, the fat yellow kayaks slide forward in the April sunlight. It feels good to be on the water again, watching Marjorie patrolling the flat beach at Boundary Bay, B.C., with Leo, the whippet. The kayaks float in three inches of water, but our thirteen-year-old niece Jocelyn has run aground, and she giggles, paddling backward to free herself.

I grew up here on the West Coast; my parents lie in a cedar-rimmed cemetery two miles away. But the Maritimes have been my home for thirty years and, truthfully, I would never have come back but for Marjorie, to whom the West Coast is as essential as air to a bird. *You couldn't leave the Maritimes,* she said, early in our courtship. *You wrap your village around you like a cloak. And I couldn't leave the West Coast.* Then don't, I said. Just add the East Coast.

*Marjorie: Just add the East Coast, he said. I hardly knew where it was. Born in Ottawa, raised in Vancouver, my idea of "east" stretched only to Montreal. Yet the home this man described lay one thousand miles beyond Quebec, on a 42.5-square-kilometre island. Isle Madame, population 4,300, at the southeast corner of Cape Breton Island.*

*Look at them out there, laughing together, my mischievous girl and my boy-hearted husband. I take a mental photograph of the two of them in this Pacific world. Tomorrow we go home to Nova Scotia; today I store images of my beloved West Coast.*

*If I could, I'd fit Jocelyn into my suitcase. She'd come, too. She loved her visit to the Maritimes last summer. Even tells my sister, "Mum, we have to move to Nova Scotia."*

Don: We migrate between oceans: three seasons in Nova Scotia, winters in B.C. I have learned to love Pacific things again: the towers of downtown Vancouver spiking upward against the snow-sugared mountains, the pink flowering of plum and cherry, the flat channel-seamed delta of the Fraser River, the sense of the Orient lying out beyond the ocean horizon.

Despite its occasional storms, this coast seems dreamy, soft, almost absent-minded. Sailboats here carry tall rigs, light sails and reliable engines, sharing the sounds and fjords with the seine boats I grew up with – white-painted and varnished, snub-nosed, at once muscular and stylish. Out here "fish" means the flashing, leaping varieties of Pacific salmon: chinook, pink, sockeye, coho, chum. At home it means the deep-feeding, slow-moving cod.

The Atlantic coast is hard, blustery, tangy with iodine. Marjorie found the Maritimes more foreign than Europe.

Marjorie: *"Tell me when to panic," I said as we drove for the first time towards his home in the village of D'Escousse, population 250. The road was abundantly lined with silver oaks and apple trees, but the second- and third-growth evergreens behind these looked to me like baby Christmas trees. Most houses were tall rectangles, many with flat roofs. No glass-flecked Vancouver stucco here: houses were either wood-shingled or vinyl-sided. Colours ranged from white to sage green and barn red; facades were either utterly plain or softened by decorative shutters and ornate fretwork – "carpenter's lace."*

*The grounds were plain, too. Few were studded by trees or bushes, and fences were blue-moon rare. Instead I saw clotheslines propped up by poles, the clothes ordered precisely along them from large to small, from those nearest the house to those farthest away, like colourful handkerchiefs in the breeze.*

*"All right, time to panic." We'd already passed through several villages – and I couldn't tell when we left one and entered another. Nonetheless, three and a half hours from Halifax, we had reached D'Escousse, an ancient French word for "a stopping place."*

*And so we stopped. Another tall house, Wedgewood blue with a flat roof. Grateful to reach journey's end, I walked into a spacious and beautifully restored home that had its first incarnation over one hundred years ago, when the very first trains were pulling into Vancouver. Isle Madame itself has been home to Europeans for almost three hundred years.*

*For me, Maritime history has catapulted out of books and into the land of now, my life. I see this history in the enormous, elaborate Victorian homes of Annapolis Royal, and hear it in the lilting accents of my neighbours. "Yiss, yiss," said one the other day, "Well, dat man's right owly. And why? Life's too short t' be mean." Many of them speak Acadian French, which relies mostly on the familiar "tu" form of address. "What's this about privacy?" laughs a friend. "We're Acadians."*

*Visitors are frequent, and mostly unannounced, and doors are never bolted. "If you lock up," say neighbours, "how would we get in?" So in they come, sometimes for a cup of tea, often to bring a small gift – a loaf of bread, still warm from the oven, or a bag of "lobster goo," hideously stinky broken shells to fertilize the garden. "How are you to-day?" asks the city girl, nervously patting her yet-uncombed hair. Invariably, cheerfully: "Oh good, dear, good. You?"*

Don: When we first lived together in B.C., I felt abandoned. Marjorie locked the doors, and only couriers came to the house. Marjorie, I said, what's the matter with people here? Don't they like each other?

But the difference is partly rural-urban, not merely east-west. I had almost forgotten the pleasures of the city. In Vancouver, we go to the symphony, see first-run films in real theatres, eat superbly in what seem like a million cosmo-politan restaurants. The city means easy access to great libraries, zoos and aquar-iums, live theatre, a dram of Laphroaig on a sun-dappled deck beside a down-town marina.

Marjorie loves food; me, I always thought of it as fuel. But on Valentine's Day she organized a feast. We went to the farmer's market and the seafood shops on Granville Island and came home with live oysters and fresh shrimp, crusty Italian bread, crisp raddichio and yellow peppers and red onions – and a succulent, operatic German chocolate dessert. Marjorie feasts us in D'Escousse, too, but she drives thirty miles to pick through a far skimpier array of ingredients.

In my youth Granville Island was an industrial district. I drove a truck down there to pick up galvanized metal for a heating company. Now it's a chic oasis of boutiques, boats, food shops, theatres, bookstores and galleries. One gal-lery is devoted to the bold art of British Columbia's two hundred native bands. There I bought Marjorie a ring to mark our happy first year of marriage. It was made by Derek Wilson, of the Haisla tribal nation, an elegant engraving of a gold hummingbird on silver.

Marjorie: *I didn't know that Nova Scotia has just one aboriginal nation, the Mi'kmaq, with whom I shared tea and talk last July at the annual Ste. Anne's Mission celebration on the Bras d'Or Lakes. In B.C., the various First Nations people I've schooled and worked with all seemed to share a common genetic gift: humour as richly contoured as the West Coast itself. The Mi'kmaq are like that, too. But I didn't know of their long-standing commitment to the Roman Catholic church, a result of five hundred years of European contact. I want to learn how Mi'kmaq traditional spirituality meshes with Christianity.*

*I'd also never heard the term "kitchen racket" until I came to Cape Breton. Last summer we had our very own kitchen racket to celebrate our marriage, a party that brought more than two hundred guests to our home. Fifty pounds of mussels, bowls of pickled herring or "Solomon Gundy." The skin of an Irish bodhrán drum warmed against the steady strike of palm and fist; its Celtic heartbeat blended with guitar, piano and a full chorus of voice. Three days passed before the final guests left. The freezer bulged with party offerings, fed us for weeks afterwards. Never in my life have I experienced so much sustained good will and merriment. Or had so many willing hands to help with a cleanup.*

Don: Free again, Jocelyn paddles by. When she visited us last summer, I organized a tour to places new to both Marjorie and Jocelyn – to the golden beaches of Prince Edward Island, and to a friend's homestead in the Island woods where the loudest sound was the drumming whir of hummingbirds in the hollyhocks and morning glory. We prowled Charlottetown, bought ice cream at the original Cows outlet, saw *Anne of Green Gables* at the Confederation Centre.

We crossed the thirteen-kilometre Confederation Bridge and drove on to Bouctouche, New Brunswick, home of the tycoon K.C. Irving and the Acadian novelist Antonine Maillet, whose works inspired a theme park on pilings out in the sluggish river. We went to the salty old German town of Lunenburg, a World Heritage Site, all curlicues and gargoyles, where the Folk Harbour Festival gave Jocelyn a taste of East Coast music. We breakfasted on a balcony overlooking Lunenburg's waterfront with its fish plants, warehouses and schooners, and photographed Jocelyn aboard *Bluenose II*.

Marjorie: *When I think of Jocelyn's visit, I remember the natural way she moved aboard Silversark, our red-sailed, black-hulled cutter, which resembles a saucy pirate vessel. No less saucy and confident was Jocelyn, when we went for an overnight sail through the island-peppered waters of Lennox Passage. Sailing came to her as if by osmosis. "That's my West Coast marine girl," I thought proudly. I'd have given a lot for her mother, a former commercial fisherman, to have seen her daughter's sure, soft tread on deck.*

*Or to have heard her explosion of giggles when we saw a yellow and red high-way sign advertising "McLobster" sandwiches. "St – stop the car!" she sputtered. "I have to take a photo." She has the photo, but we didn't try the sandwich.*

*I miss that girl.*

Don: I know some things that Marjorie misses: the fishing ports of Steveston and Ladner, the sea-girdled campus of the University of British Columbia, where both of us have studied and worked. She misses the taste of sushi and golden battered prawns, the smell of the horse barns in Southlands, the riverside trails where she rode Coqeyn, Boo, Kaber and many other horses, and where she walked with Leo. Above all, she misses her easy visits with friends and family, just as I miss my own Vancouver family – and, increasingly, Marjorie's as well.

I love the East Coast – its water-dappled landscapes, its architecture, its music, its savory language, its general snugness. I marvel at its casual assimilation of its dark and bloody history, and revel in the intimate web of family and place which cradles its people so that they are never truly at home anywhere else. After three decades, I am like that myself.

Yet though the flowering branches of my life are Atlantic, its roots are Pacific. Vancouver is a spectacular kaleidoscope, with its pagodas and minarets and geodesic domes, its log booms and exotic restaurants, its freighters clustered in the outer harbour, its sprawling air of sybaritic luxury. But beneath that kaleidoscopic splendour, Vancouver is a disconcertingly ductile place, so young and volatile that it is always becoming something else. Nova Scotia, after four hundred years, has condensed into something stable and unique, deeply rooted in the Old World and yet ineluctably situated in the New.

Marjorie: *Marriage came with one lover, two lives. And yet they balance each other, these coasts – old and new, city and village. I smile at the man in the kayak, laughing again with the girl. For us, home is always salt water, and one another.*

## LET IT SNOW, LET IT SNOW, LET IT SNOW
### D'ESCOUSSE, NOVA SCOTIA, 2003

It must be something in the water. Or perhaps mothers' milk. Maybe it's genetic. Then again, it could be nature and nurture. Only a double whammy like that could explain the unrelenting cheeriness of Cape Bretoners on the subject of weather. Even during this winter, the one that won't quit, won't moderate, won't release its icy stranglehold on most of Canada, I have never heard so many ringing tributes to the wisdom and generousity of Mother Nature. Think I exaggerate? Here's a sampling, from the past year or so on Isle Madame.

Neighbour One, as I trudge by him on the village road in February, the wind so biting my face has lost all feeling: "Beautiful day! Milder than yesterday, for sure." He has three fewer layers of clothing on than I do, and his arms are outstretched to encompass the apparently boundless beauty of the winter world around us. The four-foot hedges of snow along the edge of the road are blackening from the exhaust of cars, the dirty snow underfoot has ice beneath it. There's a dirty-looking sky above us, too, both in colour and probable intent.

"Daffodils," I reply wearily. "There are daffodils blooming on the West Coast right now."

"I saw that on the TV news last night," he laughs, "thought of you. But hey, you know what, that's not so good."

Not so good? Must be a relative concept, more so than I understood. What could be bad about soft, honey-scented air and a landscape royally rich with colour?

Neighbour One is still beaming, reveals the obvious with a wink: "Lawns, they'll be mowing their lawns about now. We don't have to."

Well, silly, ungrateful me. Thank all the Powers That Be that we don't have to breathe in the fresh, invigorating scent of newly mown grass. That would be depressing. The mere thought has my spirits deflated and my feet dragging dejectedly toward home. But wait, Neighbour One has more to add.

"And no bugs! We won't get bugs for months! Those poor guys out west."

They're the same in summer. Neighbour Two, early last July, on a chilly, teeming morning not fit for ducks, the two of us arriving at the grocery store door at the same time: "I can't believe how lucky we are." She looks beatific. Perturbing, when I look as though the unicorn and I missed passage on The Ark.

I swipe back several strands of wet, tangled hair and repeat the most confusing word of her pronouncement: "Lucky?"

Rapid nods and a sweeping hand to the pewter sky above us. "I haven't had to water my garden in over a month! Why, it's practically self-caring with all this lovely rain. Everything smells so clean and delicious. And the wells are topped right up, no worries there, either. Summer rains, they're practically romantic, aren't they?"

Other than a dazed "Uh-huh," there is no suitable response. You can't very well speak out against romance, can you?

Neighbour Three, a cousin of Neighbour Two and with her on that day, has the last word. Upbeat, of course – these two are related, after all. And born and raised in This Weather-Demented Region.

"And you know what else," she trills, "I haven't seen an earwig in days. Just too cold for them to flourish."

For me, too, I nearly wail. But I bite my churlish tongue.

A frigid summer week later, Neighbour Four is standing in line in front of me at the local post office. He is speaking not to me but to a male friend, who has already collected his mail. The friend stands near to him, yet Neighbour Four's voice is stage-bold, the tone conspiratorial, more than a little bit smug. "Ahh, these cool summer nights – they work to our advantage," says he. Now there's an interesting phrasing, I think, I wonder what exactly he –

"We can sleep well at night, and our wives want to snuggle ..." I depart the post office hastily, to the sound of happy guffaws.

Neighbour Four, when the dog-days of last summer arrived; not a second of wind, only a stone curtain of heat and mugginess: "You gotta love this! Just like the Tropics – 'cept we didn't have to travel anywhere, the heat came to us! Cheap vacation or what?" He dives back into the weirdly tepid harbour waters. Hugging a furnace might be more refreshing.

Three summers ago, and the tail end of a hurricane slams through our village of D'Escousse. Some boats drag their moorings toward the open Atlantic, bound for Ireland. Others tear free of their moorings, bounce merrily over gargantuan waves toward rocky harbour shores. The wharf is an angry animal that lurches, heaves and bucks. Our family sailboat appears to be safe on her mooring. But the other vessels will need to be retrieved. It's all I can do to stay on my feet, as I sway and stagger against the buffeting of curiously warm winds.

Neighbours One through Dozens are much more nimble-footed; they appear, in fact, to be dancing on that same mobile wharf. Cries of "Rock 'n' roll!" and "Let 'er rip!" rise above nature's shrieking orchestra. Quick shouted conferences ascertain that no one has died or been injured, so spirits soar as heaven-high as the winds. Several skippers have fired up the engines on their Cape Island vessels; soon they'll be rounding up stray boats like cowboys roping steers on the range. Male bodies are flying off the wharf, their departures punctuated by Tarzan bellows. *Ker-thump!* Their rubber boots land squarely on broad decks. Arms are held aloft like Olympic gymnasts awaiting a judge's scoring.

An exhausting day concludes late in the afternoon. The wind has eased to melodic gusts. Neighbours One through Dozens head home to hot toddies and supper: "Holy whistlin', that was a jeezly good blow ..."

You know, I love good weather as much as anyone else. It's the any-weather-is-worth-celebrating part I haven't mastered yet. However Cape Bretoners have come by this strange but laudable attitude, I now see it as an art. Takes considerable mental and spiritual agility to see the rainbow before it emerges from behind the clouds.

All the same, glad we don't get tornadoes around here. They'd close the schools and hold a three-day picnic, with live music and a lobster boil. Woe betide the Neighbour who mentions her house has blown away ...

## Fabric Ballet
### D'Escousse, Nova Scotia, 2003

Dancing colours: every week I see them – under clear skies or clouds or even in light rain or snow – in every shade and shape imaginable. Sometimes static, sometimes manic, occasionally moving in deliciously slowed motion. It's been seven years since I moved to the country and first encountered this classic art form. It's time I stopped depending on my dryer and learned to create my own fabric ballet. I know just the woman who can help me.

It's Monday morning, the day I begin learning "Outdoor Clotheslines." I am the sole student in the class that my friend and neighbour, Denise Saulnier, will teach. She is an umpteenth-generation Nova Scotian, born and raised on the "French Shore" between Yarmouth and Digby. I am a transplanted Vancouverite.

Today we both live in the village of D'Escousse, on Isle Madame, in Cape Breton.

It all began with a conversation over tea. Shyly, I shared my secret longing with my new Acadian friend. "Oh, sure," she said at first, "go ahead, use your clothesline." She paused, then added, "And if I were you, I wouldn't even worry about the laundry police."

Laundry police?

"Just kidding," she laughed. "Sort of. Besides, it's quite possible that the rules aren't as strict on Isle Madame as they are where I grew up."

Rules?

My friend chattered on, then stopped at the sight of my woebegone face. "It's all that colour and movement that gets to you, isn't it?" she said. "And the symmetry of the line, right?"

I nodded, feeling slightly embarrassed.

"You haven't done this before, have you?"

Well, yes, in a way. We did have an outdoor clothesline where I grew up at 43rd Avenue and Dunbar Street on the southwest side of Vancouver. I dimly remember sandy bathing suits and beach towels strung out on it – but not everyday clothes. Those languished down in our basement. I explained how the ropes squared the area around the washing machine. Inside, it felt as though you were in a tent, and finding your way out through the folds could be a challenge.

"Indoor clotheslines?" Her furrowed brow suggested that such a method defeated the overall purpose. Outdoor fresh and all that. She was right. Technically clean, the clothes often continued to exude a vague whiff of *eau de cellar*.

"I have no idea," I said. "And it wasn't just my family. Hardly anyone I knew used an outdoor clothesline when I was a kid. You just never saw one." Out of West Coast loyalty, I omitted the other, more likely explanation for Vancouver's dearth of outdoor clotheslines – the rains do come.

"Listen, I would try the outdoor clothesline," I said, "if I knew those damn rules you were talking about."

"Monday morning, first thing," she replied.

So here we are. No birds are singing; no birds are even awake. Regulation one: all laundry must be on the line by 10:00 a.m. Otherwise, "Well, *sloven* is a word that I've heard used," says Denise.

We are in the laundry room on the second floor of the seaside house that my husband and I live in. To reach the clothesline, all I have to do is open a window; it stretches from the house to a tree a full fifty feet away. As we did in my childhood, I have a capacious wicker basket into which I've piled the clean washing. And I've remembered my friend's stern reminder, too, that kitchen linens (dish cloths, tea towels, napkins and tablecloths) must be washed separately from personal articles (bath towels and face cloths).

I start with socks and underwear. These, as with all other items, must proceed from light to dark and from small to large. Denise takes me to task for my profligate use of clothespins (no gale blows this morning, after all) and I learn to space the pins regularly, not merely when I feel a creative urge to snap one on the line.

As instructed, I fold each piece of laundry over the line, pull it taut and pin it and, within each category, spread out the most pleasing colour gradations. The toes on the socks must be pointed in the same direction. Jeans and pants must be pinned at the waistbands, shirts at their tails (to fasten them at their shoulders is to leave unsightly tweak marks: not good form). Light items, such as sheets and pillowcases, go on the line last; quickly dried, they can be retrieved first.

By mid-morning I've met my objective and created my own fabric ballet. I am content. There is only one other question on my mind: "Who are the laundry police?"

"Family," says Denise. "When your surname matches the name of the place you live in, good luck avoiding the family laundry police. Neighbours, too. It's a village thing."

I try to imagine a Simminsville. In Canada, with the spelling of our surname, Simminsville would be a metropolis of twelve or so, pulled together from a four-thousand-mile radius. Not much of a police force. I stick with the general concept of villages, a complex reality I am slowly coming to understand.

"So the village makes the rules?"

"No, those seem to be universal across the Maritimes. Take a look around you, you'll see. By the way, great job for your first time. Next thing you know, we'll be sewing quilts, baking bread ..." She starts to laugh at her own joke until she catches the eager look on my face.

"No way, Marjorie."

I've had a good day. The folded laundry smells wonderful – and I haven't heard a single siren. But can I share two small secrets? Between you and me? My arm is sore ... from all the heave-hoing on the clothesline ... and I still love my ... dryer.

## Learning Cape Bretonese
### D'Escousse, Nova Scotia, 2003

Learning a second language is never easy. Learning a first language for the second time is even stranger. Or so it seems to me, an English-speaker from the West Coast, slowing gaining proficiency in "Cape Bretonese" ...

"Hey, Phoebe, take it easy, you'll have a coronary!"

The dog and I are out walking in the village on a hand-burning morning in January, and have stopped to tease a friend as she furiously shovels snow left and right along the short pathway from her house to the road. Phoebe is definitely energetic. And talkative.

"Lord liftin'," she pants, "shovellin's hard work. This old-style winter's making me right owly – leastways, this morning." She pauses for one raggedy breath, quirks an eyebrow. "Hadda crowd home last night, went wide open – didn't keep you'se up, did we?"

"No, didn't hear a thing."

"Good, dear, good. Thought you mighta heard my cousin, Seamus. Looked to get right savage wild, he did."

"What do you mean? Did he start a fight?"

Phoebe's extended family can be ... expressive in their emotional range.

"Only with himself, if you know what I mean. Tee-tot'ly-ossified. Told him to fill his boots, and Lord love him, didn't he just. I meant the chowder, not the rum. He's not the sharpest knife in the drawer, but he's some sweet when he's sober. And the way he was drug up, it's no wonder his head's not screwed down tight. What a sin."

"That bad, was it?" I had a fairly turbulent childhood myself. Not always easy to overcome with any measure of grace.

"Honest to God," says Phoebe emphatically. "My uncle – rest in peace all the same – kept those kids busy as a flea on a hot shovel. And my aunt – rest in peace, she was drug up just as bad – used to go like ninety, and always mad as a wet hen, too. All them kids ended up a pickle short of a jar, just from the racket 'round them."

"But Phoebe, that's awful."

Family. We all have one or three members we've wanted to set loose in an oar-less dinghy – on a strong current to the open ocean. At least for a week or two.

"Don't you worry on Seamus. He's got us now. And lucky us, we got him!" She rolls her eyes in mock exasperation, then glances back at the house and laughs. "Yiss, yiss, yiss, gotta take care of your family!"

She's back to shovelling now. The dog and I walk on, awkwardly, all extremities numb with cold by now. Phoebe's final words have a sunny resonance, though. At least, if I understood all that! If I did, then cancel the dinghy order. Phoebe has the better idea. No worries about that stout heart of hers, either.

## LOOKING LIKE A KEHOE
### D'ESCOUSSE, NOVA SCOTIA, 2003

"Member number, please." I am at our island food co-op, and the cashier's fingers are poised over the keys on the cash register. I stop the transfer of items from cart to counter and oh happy day, the number comes to me without hesitation.

The cashier's eyes are now fixed on the name read-out at the top of the register. She stares long and hard at the names glowing there, mine and my husband's.

"Wrong number," she says.

"No, it's right," I say, smiling. "That's us." From her expression of disbelief, you'd think I was claiming to be the Queen of Sheba. She nonetheless begins sliding the items across the scanner. Just a few groceries today. We'll be tallied up soon and then I can take one impatient dog, waiting in the car, to the beach for a walk. Ah, that'll be grand.

"Forty-three sixty-eight," says the cashier. She is still looking at me suspiciously, though her tone is pleasant. I hand over the exact change – everything is going right today – and wait for her to give me the receipt. As she does her eyes suddenly brighten. Puzzle solved, says the expression.

"You're one of the Kehoe girls, aren't you?"

Oh boy, here we go again.

"No," I say firmly. "I am not."

Now she's wide-eyed and defiant in pose, one hand on her hip, head on a tilt. "Are you sure?"

Maybe I should just give up and join the clan. This must be the twentieth time in the past two years I've said no to a question like this. Mind you, I've never had someone disbelieve me – or at least express the disbelief.

The query reverberates in the air. I guess I have to say something. I have a a feeling she won't let me leave if I don't.

"I have three sisters; two live in Ottawa, one in B.C. We are not Kehoes, by birth, marriage or chance. The Kehoes are a lovely family, but not mine." As I walk away I see the cashier still shaking her head. No need to lie, I can almost hear her say.

A brutal easterly wind slams against the shores of the beach where the dog and I go next. Heedless, our hound trots along happily; I walk on a slant, shoulders hunched up to block the wind from my bare neck. My thoughts are active. Mostly I think about the complexities of being a West Coast transplant, and my apparent resemblance to one of the longest-established families on Isle Madame.

It's been centuries since the first Irish Kehoes came to the island and settled in greatest numbers in an area called Rocky Bay. Some of my forebears – Simminses, Beauforts, O'Flaherties, Atkinsons and Glasses, the only names I remember – settled in Ontario in the early nineteenth century. Your basic early-Canadian Anglo grouping of Irish, Scot and English. Who never came near the Maritimes. Or so the family stories went.

Out of nowhere, I think about the movie *Six Degrees of Separation*, which maintained all the world's people could find someone they knew in common in no more than six circles of acquaintanceship and circumstance. However, they would not necessarily share blood ties.

Growing up in B.C., I would periodically try to lay claim to one or another of my ancestral groups. One month I'd be keen to align myself with the British (usually after reading an Enid Blyton novel, where the kids all had adventures and were always eating weird and wonderful stuff), and the next month it would be Irish (so tragically romantic and didn't they have the most beautiful Thoroughbred hunters?).

"You're no more British or Irish than you're Yugoslavian," my father would say to me bluntly. He'd add, after noting my disappointment, "You're seventh-generation Canadian. Be proud of that." (Dad's questionable math added four generations on my mother's side and three on his, for a total of seven.) I was an adult before I fully understood that his passion for Canada came in large part from a deep-seated loathing of the British class system, under which our family apparently suffered. He also, plainly and vocally, loved what he perceived as the physical hardiness and spiritual generosity of Canada's peoples, both First Nation and immigrant. The fact that I may or may not have resembled my paternal great-grandmother Charlotte Pringle O'Flahertie (just a wee bit Irish) was not of the slightest interest to him, and thus not to the child that was me. Now I don't know what to think or feel about the subject.

The bitter wind has not let up, and oblivious dog or no, we're going home now. Even Canadian-born, there are limits to my hardiness.

"It happened again," I call up the stairs to my husband's office. Footsteps come down the hall, then, from the top of the stairs, "What happened?"

"I'm a Kehoe again."

"Hang on, I'll be right down." My husband finds these stories terribly amusing. But this one has him doubled up.

"No, no," he gasps between bouts of laughter, "you've got it all wrong. Don't you remember what my old Kehoe buddy said? It's not that you look like them, it's that somewhere along the line, a very prolific Simmins passed through Rocky Bay!"

You know, this day has gone thoroughly pear-shaped. I'm still frozen from my beach walk, thoroughly confused in mind and spirit, and a reputed liar. To top it off, my husband now intimates that my possible connection to an island family may be from the wrong side of the blanket.

"No," I say eloquently. Long pause, then: "We're not going there."

"All right," says my husband, momentarily sober again, "then you explain it." I can't. So instead, I argue.

"I'm not tall." I think jealously of the tall Kehoe women I've met. You don't need much imagination for the word Viking to come to mind.

"Neither are all of them. There's a shorter branch of the family – just like you."

"I don't dance till I drop." The women and men dance like cast members of *Riverdance*.

"Well, you're out of shape at the moment."

Darn, that one backfired. Try again. I return to the basic premise: "But how is it I look like them, exactly? I don't see it."

"Listen, it's not an exact sort of thing. It's more of a gestalt, or general similarity. Fair hair and the colouring for sure. Celtic colouring definitely. Or a strain of, anyway."

"So why can't I be Black Irish? You know, with blue-black hair, milk-white skin and violet eyes. I'd claim that in a heartbeat."

"Happily, you are what you are." He's laughing again. "Which suits me fine. Me darlin' girl, I've always thought the Kehoe women brightened the landscape."

It is time, possibly, for a fit of Irish temper. Perhaps a flat-out gale.

## "*Marjorie Sightings*"
### Halifax, Nova Scotia, July 2013

"*Marjorie sightings* – did I dream up that phrase, or did someone really say it?" I am phoning one of the funniest people I know, on any coast, anywhere, from my home in the city of Halifax, to hers in the village of Arichat, Cape Breton. I do this because I have a sneaking suspicion …

Murielle immediately starts to laugh, a sound that starts girlish high and giggles down to toasty mid-range. "Oh yeah, it's real, and I said it! Why?"

"Well, sometimes I think about those first years in Cape Breton – and I can't remember the details of an event, only the phrases connected to them. Then I actually wonder if those are real, or something I made up. I am a writer, after all. And then I just have to know for sure! So, *Marjorie sightings*, tell me again – what was that all about?"

"Well, it started at Claire's Café. A bunch of us were having coffee, and someone says, 'Has anyone seen her yet?' And we say no, not yet. You know how it is, we wanted to know what you looked like." She has cracked up again.

"Muri*elle*! What did you think – that I had two heads and a peg leg?" I can't believe it, seventeen years later and I still feel a flush of embarrassment: strangers staring at me, sizing me up – and me totally unaware. City people think they are invisible. In my own books, I was just Josephine Person. Not in a village. Here I was interesting, a new person in the community. That gives everyone something to talk about. Until the next newcomer comes in, of course.

Welcome to village – and island – life. Any ol' where, in small town Canada. *The things I didn't know – thank goodness!*

"No," resumes Murielle, "we knew you were normal, we were just curious. We'd already heard you were a lot younger than Don, and had a funny skinny dog."

"Funny skinny dog! My beautiful Leo?"

"Think about it – how many whippets had ever come to Isle Madame over the years, hmmm?" It's true, there were lots of Labrador retrievers on Isle Madame, used for hunting ducks or simply as family dogs, and a fair number of small "lap-dogs" (shih tzus or terriers) and every-sized crossbreeds. Some wandered the village and took themselves for swims in the chill waters along the local beach. Others accompanied their humans on daily walks. As in the city, an unfortunate few languished at the ends of ropes, rarely off their properties. On the island's only sheep farm, working dogs such as border collies and one livestock guard dog, a fluffy white Maremma, who loved people and loathed coyotes, could be seen earning their living. But there were no sighthounds – dogs that hunt and pursue game by sight rather than by scent – no greyhounds, Afghans, Irish wolfhounds, Scottish deerhounds and the medieval like. Not a whippet to be seen ... for many miles in all directions.

Oblivious me and my sculpted racing hound: I guess we did make for good gossip.

"Can you believe it," I say to Murielle, "I used to put my lipstick on to go to the post office, just across the street from us. My mother always said, 'Put on your lipstick before going out into public.'" The village of D'Escousse, population 250 in a good year, with no sidewalks and modest, mostly underground commerce had become my "public." I rarely saw anyone on my short walks.

"Is this the 'Dunbar thing' that Don is always going on about – keeping up appearances and all that?"

"Well, kind of." For him, the phrase is shorthand for bourgeois and straitlaced. For me, it represents the good and predictable parts of my childhood, of which there were many. I loved my early schools – Kerrisdale Annex and Kerrisdale Elementary – and the thoroughly nice kids and superb teachers in them. I enjoyed swimming at local pools and playing with my friends at their homes or (when quiet) mine. I even went to the United Church on Sundays with one of my school friends and her family, for over a year. Our house was large and comfortable, filled with works of art and books. When our complicated, loving family worked well, it was a joy. Continuity. I inhaled it when I could.

There's no denying that Don and I experienced two very different Dunbar Street raisings. Don came to the neighbourhood in 1941, as a four-year-old. I came to it in 1963, also as a four-year-old. Our homes were exactly twenty blocks apart: his at 23rd and Dunbar and mine at 43rd and Dunbar. The boy next door, we often joked. In fact we were almost exactly a generation apart: the same year he got married, I was born. But even in the wobbly and wild 1970s, my growing up years, Vancouver still had a conservative, judgemental underbelly. Don's Vancouver, of the 1950s, was far worse: rigid, racist and unapologetic about touting the mores of the dominant white Christian culture. This suited restless and adventurous Don ... not one bit.

"Dunbar is a state of mind," I say to Murielle finally.

"The way Cape Breton is, but different?"

"Yeah," I say, "different."

"But rules, just like here?"

"Definitely." But if you break the rules in Cape Breton ... no one cares. The rules are more for Born-Theres, anyway. For Come-From-Aways, they just want to know what you're all about, because you might be interesting, or have something new to add to the mix, which could be useful or fun. After that, they leave you alone. Conforming to their ways is not an issue.

Aloud I say, "I think Cape Bretoners actually like different, a lot."

"See, you were perfect."

"Muri*elle!*"

But she's on a roll now. "Remember how pissed you were when I gave you that nickname?"

The Drama Queen. I was surprised when she came up with it, thought at first it was an insult – as in you are a melodramatic pain in the backside. But sharp-edged teasing is not Murielle's way. What she meant was exactly what she saw: theatrical Marjorie taking the mickey out of herself, all for the sake of a good shared laugh and a fun "performance" for her friends. If something about my new life in the country confused, worried or startled me – I'd make a joke about it. I tried not to judge and tried harder to dig out deeper understandings. Sometimes I did well – sometimes I didn't. Murielle always encouraged me to slow my judgements by adding the context about peoples' lives that I, new to the place, couldn't know. But first, I'd enjoy a good squawk about whatever I was trying to figure out.

"Well, yeah – the drama bit, it's the way I am." Anything for a laugh. Turbulent childhoods have their uses.

"Yeah, and we're fine with that. *Really*." She's laughing again, enjoying an unexpected opportunity to "torment" me, as they are fond of saying on Isle Madame. "You're all that and a bag of chips!" We ignite in laughter, match to the gas as always.

In the end, I felt pleased that Murielle "saw" me with that moniker. I liked the inclusion, too. Silver Donald Cameron, Drama Queen Marjorie. Now we both had Cape Breton nicknames.

As for Marjorie sightings, if I and my narrow tan-and-white hound made anyone smile or even diverted them briefly – from yard or housework, the unending care of children or elders, the column of numbers that wouldn't add up on a computer screen – fine by me. *Not a word of a lie*, as the islanders say. And as long as I have my lipstick on.

## 18

# OF CHILDREN AND MAKING IT RIGHT

FEBRUARY 16, 2011, HALIFAX, NOVA SCOTIA

As of tomorrow, I will be fifty-two years old. There doesn't seem to be a single thing one can say about aging that hasn't been said ad nauseam. All the same, I am as startled as anyone else to have tipped into my fifties. I am no longer, as my friend Denise also wryly says of herself, "one of the smooth ones." I try to ignore aging the way my mother did, as though it were a noisy housefly to be batted aside, and try to make it as irrelevant as my father did, a man who never actually grew old in outlook or responsiveness, but did, as my oldest sister said, "wear out." I am hoping that my genetic legacy will make me live every moment of my life as committedly as they did.

Genetic legacy. On my sad days, I tell myself that I was too stupid to propagate – an activity those with even the lowest IQs manage, along with those from every other range of intelligence. On my angry days, I list off the barriers to procreation and produce an impressive list of why nots – beginning and ending with I didn't want to be a mother on my own, without a partner, dead broke and struggling. I'd been a child pretty much on my own, with both parents overwhelmed by life events and choices, and I wasn't in a hurry to relive those feelings of isolation and desolation from the other side.

*Right, add coward to the list.*

On my wondering days, I know that I *think too much* and imagined scenarios that might never have occurred. I have seen so much hurt in the relations between parent and child, so many wretched strains and betrayals. I have seen these generally, not just in my own personal spheres.

Oddly, one of the more obvious possibilities to explain my childlessness really wasn't a factor: my sister Karin was mentally ill, but I never believed in my bones I'd see her dark blue eyes again in the face of my own child. There are times that come and go in a life and then perhaps hover, threatening to return. Others you just know are truly gone. *I'd done my time with mad shadows.*

On my calm days I remember my deep appreciation of calm – and quiet, order and predictability. This is not the world of children. Every calm day I have is like the very first, ever: I explore the parameters with a wondering, grateful heart.

These then are the reasons I think on, when I awake some mornings with a confused heart. *Where in God's name are my children, the family of my own making?* My children were the stuff of endless hours of imaginings, their names all chosen, listed in the back of my journals from age fifteen on. Countless dreams, too. I even felt I knew their foibles and fancies, long before actualization. The girl would love horses and dogs, the boy not as much. He preferred birds, camping and any pastime on the water. The youngest danced through the world, had trouble with numbers and linear logic. All would love each other and be small, solid worlds to each other, knowing the incalculable gift of siblinghood. All would sing well and unlike me, a self-taught guitarist, would learn to read and even write music. They would play instruments of every sort – and play them well. They would be safe, loved, delighted in, by two adults who lived adult lives of moderate tedium and contentment. And I would teach them, as Mum taught me, about *Roy G. Biv.*

*Do you see that rainbow?* Mum asked me, when I was very young, the only child not in school yet. She pointed to the southwest, and a bright-dark sky over the mouth of the Fraser River. *Oh,* I breathed in answer, my gaze aligned with hers, *oh yes I see it.*

She smiled. *Can you tell me the names of the colours in the rainbow?* I was lost in the deep pleasure of the place where green meets blue in the rainbow arc, did not answer her. *There's an easy way to remember the colours*, she said, *Roy G. Biv*. I didn't understand and stayed quiet. I thought Roy G. Biv was a man I hadn't met, but would, and he would explain the rainbow to me, as my mother apparently could not. She stroked my thick, wavy hair off from my face, stroked away the questions in my eyes, said with a smile, *roygbiv is a way to remember red, orange, yellow, green, blue, indigo and violet – and there's your rainbow, every colour in it.*

*Roy G. Biv,* I said, syllables molasses-slow, for I never saw the mnemonic any other way, *it's funny!* Mum's eyes widened – she suddenly saw the name, too, I am sure – and she laughed with me. *It is funny – but it works!* Her laugh stopped and her face became eager: *Do you know why I wanted you children? Because I wanted to show you the world – all its wonders and beauties. I feel so lucky I can do this.* She looked so happy, was so happy, there was no doubt, in that extended moment of colour and companionship. *Will you remember roygbiv?* she asked and laughed a brook-pretty laugh.

Yes, I will.

When my mother was a little girl, she dreamed not of being a mother but of being a lion tamer. She was also born under the astrological sign of Leo, symbolized as a lion. Her emotions, too, could be as explosive as a wild creature's. Yet as fiercely loving and committed to her children as my mother was, she also voiced a steady stream of contradictions to me from the time I was very young. Smart women didn't have to have children – or perhaps only one; that way they could get ahead in the world. *But you're smart and you had four; you had a hard but fulfilling life.* Children brought unimagined joy – and unbearable pain. *Yes, I know, but we all suffered, as a family, didn't we, and healed, as best we could – didn't we?* Doting grandparents were pathetic – she had no interest in being a grandmother like that. *I don't understand – you love your three grandchildren, and cherish the imaginary games, laughter and intensely close bond you share with Zoë's daughter, Jocelyn, who lives close by.* If a woman can't afford a child, she shouldn't have one, ever. *But you pulled off a miracle and looked after us – don't women do this every day around the world – some in families, some on their own?*

Considering my mother's life, none of these statements and the other harsher ones she made are surprising. But her vehemence made my heart skip beats at times, and along with my own reservations, helped to permanently suspend thoughts about single motherhood as an option for me.

Sometimes I think about a cartoon in *The New Yorker* I cut out once. A woman sits bolt upright in bed in her New York penthouse, husband at her side: *Damn it, George, I knew I forgot something – children.* In spite of everything, I found the cartoon amusing. I have even flippantly used it as a party joke, when well-meaning women ask if I have children and I need a laugh to change the subject.

Mostly I have come to accept that I just couldn't Make It Right, couldn't make the complexities of building a family come together in a package that made sense to me.

If there had been one hopeful beginning, with even the most meagre underpinnings of joy, however temporary – then perhaps I would have a family of my own. Without a glimpse of rainbow, I was paralyzed, could not look up and over to a future with cleared skies.

You couldn't make it perfect, suggests my husband, with deep sympathy and understanding of the woman he married. No one can, but you thought it was an option.

Yes, I truly did.

Don says I am hard on myself – harder than most people are on themselves, especially when it comes to the major decisions I've made in my life. You keep wanting to rewrite them, he says, give them better endings. Can't a decision just be a decision – made in the very best faith and knowledge at the time? Can't you ease up on yourself just a little?

*I have*, I tell him, even defensively some days. *I am much better now than when I met you. Why, I am a regular little self-cheerleader now – Miss Cheerywinky!*

He laughs at the nickname I gave myself for when I am grumpy, but won't be deflected. You are better, he says, and you know it. Better all the time, too. MacTavish and I know these things. We've taken note. You don't even kick and thrash in your sleep any more. Or talk in your sleep. Quite civilized, really.

He makes me smile. He makes me see myself as I am, not as I was. This is the air I need to breathe now. Life can't be rewritten. Only new chapters bring change, new chances to Make It Right in the moment, not in retrospect. I still have trouble living with imperfections of any sort, but *not as much.*

Self-forgiveness is a curious creature. It darts in and out of hedgerows whippet-fast and tires me out some days. Other days I run as fast as it does, tackle it right at the ankles: *Gotcha.*

Yet other days I remember my dad's eyes shining with excitement, even in the last hard year of his life: *Marjorie, believe me, the best is yet to come.*

I believe he is right.

# 19

## CONTENTMENT

*FEBRUARY 18, 2011, HALIFAX, NOVA SCOTIA (E-MAIL)*

Dear Don

I dislike you being gone. Such a lovely birthday day and evening with you, and then, poor man, you are up and gone so early this morning on the trip to Toronto. I felt sad eating my breakfast alone at the dining room table, itself still festive with flowers, candles and a pretty tablecloth. I'll return to it in a moment, to write some thank you notes for birthday gifts.

Thank you, dear Don, for all the wonderful presents in the past few days. My flame-tipped roses are still fresh and surprisingly fragrant for a wintertime bouquet. I love the card with the little girl hugging her horse and I love the barn coat! Imagine, I can fit a size small again! I'm already into the Sheltie stationery and I am embarrassingly happy with the Sheltie night light! The donation to The Coming Home Society feels so right and so good. Makes me feel I've touched my West Coast world and maybe, if we are lucky, the life of a Coast Salish woman who wants to come home again, to heal and grow strong again.

Add to all this the feast we had last night ... and I could cry for all the cherishing. You are my best gift of any season, any time. I think it's hilarious that between the cocktails and appetizers and the lobster main course, we slipped away to have a nap – is this our life lately, or what! I am tired today, too, though hope to have at least the morning at the computer writing.

We'll have the champagne when you're home again. Have an excellent week of business and family time. Give my love to *toute la gang Chez Cameron(s)* and take lots for yourself. MacTavish and I miss you already. We will both be properly groomed when you return, I in for a haircut today, and MacT to Sharon's scissors sometime next week.

Love and hugs,
M & M


## FEBRUARY 25, 2011, HALIFAX, NOVA SCOTIA

Don will be home around midnight. He left our truck at the airport so I don't have to pick him up. My night vision is pretty much shot – though oddly, I still don't need reading glasses. I avoid driving at night as much as I can. It's not too bad on city roads, because they are well-lit. It's the long, black highways I find frightening to navigate. I have no depth perception and "lose" the road at every inky bend. Headlights seem to pierce right through my skull via my tender middle-aged eyeballs. I have glasses that help with light sensitivity, but only modestly so. I am grateful to Don for getting home on his own steam. MacTavish and I will be glad to be a family trio again. We all do best, I think, when we are together. Being together also makes these dark winter days easier to manage.

I am tired of snow and ice – even though this winter didn't really start in earnest until January. I've been a Maritimer long enough to know that a short winter seems to make spring come faster. The problem is, the Vancouver-raised girl will always look for spring flowers earlier than she has any business doing so, on this coast at any rate. Adding to my impatience is the fact that I also planted lots of new bulbs this year. I can't wait to see the new tulips, daffodils and narcissi, in the front and back garden. Being a Maritimer means being more patient in the wait for spring. Translation: *All in good time. Don't whinge.*

I am glad for the years I spent as a deckhand on my fisherman's troller and for the later years writing about the commercial fishing industry. If anything taught me not to whinge, it was being around fishermen. Their work is heavy, dangerous, bloody and unending. This makes a person *want* to complain, as unendingly. Instead, if you're smart enough, you focus on the other side of the fishing life, the one of privilege and extreme beauty. It is all around you.

*Roy G. Biv* again: double rainbows at dawn, their vivid colours set against a gold and pink northern sky. Dall's porpoises playing at the bow of the vessel, wake-bubbles created on their long noses and skimming back along their shiny black and white bodies. The lingering, homey smell of bacon, eggs and toast in the cabin, on a filthy-skied rainy morning. Each time you step back in the cabin from the deck, you feel safe, nurtured. The oil stove is always warm, you can make more coffee or toast if you want. The seas you've travelled over are more shades of grey, green and blue than you knew existed; you never tire of the waves' frilled edges. You make stacks of sandwiches, find the treat cookies under the galley berth and under the deck hatch, the last of the fresh fruit, now bruised but no matter. Ginger ales all around. The food is inhaled, the skipper never even leaves the cockpit. For most of the day.

Later, much later, standing thigh-deep in pink salmon on the starboard side of the deck, laughing at the absurdity of not being able to move to my cleaning trough, not being able to move, at all. Deckhand Two, on the port side, has made it to his cleaning trough, sings a victory song. Singing is helpful. Both of us know at midnight, the day is long from over. The deck lights are an eerie green-white in the darkness of a Pacific night; the fish blood smells metallic, is the only scent in the world now. My hands and feet are freezing and my face is going numb. None of it matters. We're making a good dollar for an honest day's work. I kill as fast and as kindly as I can; it's not something I ever wanted to do, but there is satisfaction in competence. Salmon are delicious. I can kill for this taste, this money. Apart from waitressing, it will be the only good money I ever make in my lifetime. I think somehow I knew that, as

I sang along with Deckhand Two. Behind us, in the cockpit pens, my fisherman is also cleaning fish. His hands are a blur.

Later, latest yet, those same two muscular arms lift me off my feet and carry me into the cabin. My knees buckle as my fisherman pulls off my wet boots and tugs off my blood-streaked rain gear. "Can you manage the rest?" he smiles, patting my jeans. I nod, too tired to speak. "You and Gordie did well," he says, his own face grey with fatigue beneath the windburn. "You especially. It was a big day. We dressed over eight hundred pinks and sockeye." He nods at the only stateroom, where I sleep in solitary splendour; the men sleep in the fo'c's'le below. "I wish I could sleep with you – but it's not right, not with someone else aboard – do you understand?"

*You and Gordie did well – you especially.* I nod at him with happy eyes. And yes, I understand. There will be other nights.

There were. I am glad for that.


## FEBRUARY 26, 2011, HALIFAX, NOVA SCOTIA

People do leave, and do come home. It makes my heart pound sometimes. I just love that second part.

I was holding MacTavish against my chest in bed last night when I heard Don's footsteps on the walkway by the side door to the house. Tavish was off like a shot, sounding his full-on alarm bark. "S'okay, Tav, it's just Don," I said uselessly, getting up myself. *It's Don, it's Don, let me see him –*

He looked fatigued but was cheerful and palpably glad to be home. "It was a great trip," he said several times, between bear hugs to me and smaller hugs to MacTavish, "but busy, lots going on." This is Don-speak for a trip that would have most people on their knees whimpering for clemency. I come from a family of workers, and all my friends are hard workers, too. I've had exasperating and dysfunctional boyfriends, but never a lazy one. I've even flattered myself in this regard. But I mostly think I didn't really comprehend the term *work* until I met Don. When he decides to focus and *produce*, he is an awesome force. That he does this almost every day of his life is hard to explain to people. Questions such as How's Don, what's he up to these days? are difficult to answer succinctly. Ah, do you mean his books, or his newspaper column or his real estate businesses or his new Green Interview initiative or his latest round of speeches or his new novel or his corporate writing projects or – gulp – his business and sailing plans for the future?

Mostly what I have observed with wonder are his twin abilities of divergent and convergent thought. I am queen of the divergent thinkers – you want ideas, lots of them, on anything and everything? I am your girl – but it's only been since knowing Don that I've understood more about the functions of convergent thinking. *Bear down on the point,* as my father used to say. Ideas are indeed wonderful – but they must be *implemented or enacted* for greatest exposure and effect. This is how books come to be published, not merely dreamed about or stuck at a first draft. This is how small businesses actually give back, don't just sound good in discussions or look good on the drawing board. This is how boats are built, and boats are sailed. This is how dreams about sailing six thousand miles to the Bahamas and back actually occur for ...

... a man, a woman ... and the bravest whippet in all the land.

*Welcome home*, I said. *We've missed you.* The "we" looks a little different, feels so much the same, for ...

... a man, a woman ... and a brilliant Shetland sheepdog, yet to be tested on a long voyage.

## PRAIRIE DREAMSCAPE
### ESSAY WRITTEN FOR DON'S MOTHER, WHO I NEVER MET
### WRITTEN WHILE CRUISING ON OUR SAILBOAT TO THE BAHAMAS, 2005

"While you're on your hind legs prancing," says my husband, smiling widely and extending his empty coffee mug in my general (sitting) direction across the galley table from him.

Before I have a chance to inquire about what surely must be a newly broken ankle, he's already retrieved the coffee thermos from its safe spot in the galley sink and is filling both our mugs.

"I haven't used that expression in years," he says, still smiling, though gently now, memories warming his eyes. "Pretty silly, isn't it?"

"No," I say. "I like it. Most of us just say, 'While you're up …?' and leave it at that. Hind legs prancing is more fun. Your mum, right?"

"Who else?"

It's true, my husband's mother, who I never met, seemed to have a revolving and plentiful supply of amusing expressions. Her three sons still use many of them.

"We'll do our little best."

"Time to call it half a day."

"Well, I'll love you and leave you."

"That's why I'm so much fun to be with."

And my three favourites: "You crazy fool, you'll kill us all" (about bad drivers); "Let joy be unconfined" (said with heavy irony); and "We must do with things as things will do with us" (expressing calm amidst confusion).

I wish I could have seen the look on her face as she offered up these cheery or florid sayings, though I almost can when I look at the face of her eldest son, my husband, as the side of his mouth twitches with a suppressed laugh and his eyes shine with right-there-ness of enjoying his mother's voice and peppery delivery.

They disagreed, and often, he tells me, about how to live life the best one could. But I know from photographs how similar their smiles were and how warmly they exchanged these smiles. Lack of love was not an issue. As for the rest, they both "did their little best" to respect one another's choices. Every turn of phrase shared with me is the most evocative and immediate way I will ever come to know my husband's mother.

Like all of us, she was an adult for many more years than a child. And yet my most enjoyable imaginings of her are as a child and were given to me after my first visit to Manitoba, three autumns ago. It was there, just outside of the small town of Treherne, that my husband's mother grew up. She was the second oldest of eight children. They were farm children, hard-working and kept relentlessly busy by parents who were more so.

Over them all, sun like clarified butter shone from a blue expanse of prairie sky. As vivid were stretching acres of golden grain, swaying in the breezes. Smaller flower and vegetable gardens were tended by nimble young fingers. Chickens and cows were fed, eggs and milk retrieved. Horses were groomed, harnessed and worked, and in stolen moments, I like to think, ridden bareback, their summer coasts glossy and hot against bare child legs.

It is impossible to think of large families and farms and not think of food. From the screen door leading to the kitchen, there must have come the hunger-stirring smells of baking bread, meat stews, applesauce with nutmeg, the tart tang of pickles and the simmering, ruby richness of jams. At the supper table, prayers for health, of gratitude, for rain and sun as needed and God willing, amen. Let the wheat harvest be bountiful this year. Now sit straight and elbows off the table, thank you.

In the winter, the vast flat world turned white and frigid. Slim boys and girls became rounded by many layers of clothing. Heads were haloed by steam; prairie dragons, each hard breath pouring more smoke into the air. As though charmed, the children were drawn to the shining, wickedly pointed icicles that hung from the house eaves. The taller boys broke off the narrower icicles, placed them one by one in the ring of mittened palms. All the children sucked and crunched on the dripping bounty until their mouths and tongues were numb. Then to school. On the way home, the children walked even faster, with hopeful thoughts of cocoa or steaming chicken broth awaiting them at home.

These are the things I think of when I imagine my husband's mother's growing-up years in Manitoba.

The autumn Don and I visited Treherne, the prairie-scape shone a dappled gold and green. I soon learned that clusters of graceful elms announced homesteads.

"There it is," he said. And there indeed it was, the white clapboard house I'd seen in photo albums, its immediate perimeter shaded by elms and hazel trees. The house even had a name, Hazeldell, and was still a family home, occupied by a distant cousin of Don's.

The photos I'd seen were wedding photos. Don's mother married a Prairie man, though they met on the West Coast of Canada and would later return there. As I remembered the photos, he wore a well-tailored suit, his expression lit by pride. She was petite, and her figure trim. The dress was feminine but not fussy, and a pretty shawl added a sweet, old-fashioned touch. Her long hair was worn as a Scandinavian woman might, in sleek braids around her head. All around the pair were family. There are bands of shadow on some of the beaming faces. A sunny day then, which made skin warm, eyes narrow and the air fragrant with blooms.

I've been so lost in my meandering thoughts of long ago that when I look up, I am startled to see the world beyond our cabin windows dipping and rising. No house this, though our boat has been home for over six months. We are a long way from Treherne. From Canada for that matter. Even from the North American mainland.

"Time to climb the wooden hill," says my husband, yawning. Another saying of his mother's, but I can't remember what this one means. I lift an eyebrow.

"You know, wooden hill," he repeats. "The staircase to the second floor, where people sleep at night." He waggles his eyebrows back at me, points a finger toward the boat's overhead. He looks so goofy I can't resist playing the straight guy.

"I think it's too cold to sleep on the deck." Wouldn't that be comfortable. I pause, still straight-faced, trying to remember yet one more of his mother's expressions. It comes to me on the downside of a giggle. "But have it your own foolish way, if you must."

We will, of course, kip down below in the V-berth, warm but closed off from the stars. If I could choose, I'd ask for a dreamscape of cobalt prairie sky, filled with tumbling cumulus clouds. Perhaps I'd see a young girl with her hair in braids, tied with ribbons, sitting in the shade of an elm, a book in her lap. More likely she's working in the garden or in the kitchen, spooning blackberry jam into Mason jars. Maybe she's resting, too, under a talc-soft cotton quilt that she and her sisters pieced together. She could be dreaming of becoming a teacher, a wife, and a mother. Tonight, Miss Hazel Robertson is simply a young girl in a family of ten, listening to the last of the cricket song through the open bedroom window.

## FEBRUARY 28, 2011, HALIFAX, NOVA SCOTIA

A pleasant weekend and so good for we three – Don, Tav and me – to be together again, after Don's week in Toronto. Saturday morning dawned brilliantly sunny, with a new layering of feathery snow atop previous snowfalls. I shovelled our walkways and stairs before breakfast, searching, and failing to find, a word or words to describe the smell of snow. Two days later, on another sunny morning, I have decided that snow does not have a smell, only sensations of cold in the nose and on the face that seem that they should be smells.

There are no ambiguities to snow as a visual entity. Nor do there seem to be finite expressions of it. Sunlit snow offers tiny gems to the eyes. The colours are pinpricks and shine in iridescent blankets over yards, parklands, hillsides. Swirling snowflakes are small starred universes, set free from the sky. Fluffy snow demands to be scooped up and marvelled at, each thumb-brush revealing ancient, lacy mysteries.

*You see? No two snowflakes are the same – isn't that a miracle?*

Mum? Is that you?

Her words are not my first memory of the world. But snow might be.

940 Riverside Drive, Ottawa, Ontario – I am so bundled up I can barely see. The hood of my snowsuit covers my head and is tugged down over my forehead. A woolen scarf is wrapped once around my neck, once over my mouth, then tied to one side on my shoulder. In terms of skin that meets the frigid air, it would be my nose and eyelids and nothing else. I am two or perhaps three years old. Likely three, as I am able to stumble along unaided and I quiver with the intent to travel further forward. I want to go to – *the world out there, in the glittering snow*. I stand on the big wraparound porch of our riverside home, at the top of many stairs down to the yard. I am aware of nothing but snow-desire. Snow

with colour-glints like the crystal candle holders on our dining room table, when the sun strikes their sharply cut angles: royal blue, turquoise, tangerine, yellow and green. Snow that I will put in my mouth, throw in the air. Snow that I will form into clumped together shapes of almost-balls. Snow that will make my wool mittens soggy and hands numb almost immediately.

All this I want, desperately, inchoately, standing at the top of the stairway looking down on rainbow sprinkles in the snow. Siblings or parents may be near me, must be near me – but I do not sense them or want them. I step down to the first stair –

– and seem to be over my head in snow. Did I slide down to the deeper snow at the bottom of the staircase? Was the snow on that first stair so deep I got lost? Did I just slip and land on my own bottom on that first stair? I think I am laughing. I know that caring arms have scooped me up. As I am pulled up I see more rainbows, caught in the line of icicles along the roof edge. I reach out with eager hands, snow forgotten, to the closest icicle. *Oh please!* There is a tiny sun captured within the icy dagger. If I suck the icicle – will it be cold or hot?

*A winter day in Ottawa, fifty years ago.*

I have a companion memory to this one, from the same period – perhaps even the same winter. I visit the memory like a friend who always has a kind word at hand and makes the perfect cup of tea.

A low winter sun in the Ottawa Valley shines slantwise on a black and white world. The snow is packed smooth and firm on the country laneway but is impassable in the fields that bracket it. Beyond these, on the perimeter of all that can be known by a three-year-old, are Dutch elms and birches, tall black sticks that fringe the open country acres.

"Are we ready?" Dad's question is exhaled in a puff of cold-smoke; a real cigarette adds to the smoke-wisps around him. His voice is excited. He loves adventures.

"Almost, Richard, give me a moment." Mum must be "counting her chicks" – all four children are aboard the horse-drawn wagon, though our bodies are mostly obscured under piles of wool blankets. Minutes before, we'd been running, hollering and playing in the snow, nicely toasty from the exertion. Now we are stationary, silent and freezing cold. Mum tugs a blanket here, a blanket there, to cover us better, turns to Dad, says, "Yes, we're ready." Dad helps her into the wagon. She comes straight to me, which is what I expect and want. I am the youngest.

"Cold?"

In answer I hold out my arms. "Wait," she smiles and settles herself crosswise in the wagon, back against one wooden side. She lifts me with one arm and with the other, opens her fur coat and tucks me on her lap. She closes the heavy beaver-fur coat tightly around us. The instant heat from our two bodies touching is exactly what I needed. The cold is so intense it isn't a feature of the world, it is the world, hard and implacable. Now that I am not focused on it as much, the world is friendly and of great interest again. The smell of the two draft horses – sharpish sweat, exhalations of grain-breath – makes me want to be nearer to them, place my hands on anything furry I can reach. I can smell the leather of their harness, too, honeyed by saddle soap. One of the horses whinnies, stomps an impatient hoof. A shiver of bells rises in the air. For some reason this breaks a tension of sorts, makes all of us laugh. We are excited, too.

"Are we ready?" This time it is the driver of the wagon, the man who owns the sleigh-ride business. Dad sits beside him, in the front seat. Dad turns behind to us, Mum nods and six voices shout, "Yes!"

The horses surge forward over a broad ribbon of white, the sound of bells marking each step.

*A winter day in the Ottawa Valley, five decades ago.*

## 20

## CITY LIFE; COASTAL LIVES

*MARCH 1, 2011, HALIFAX, NOVA SCOTIA*

I started painting the kitchen yesterday. I have one task finished, three coats of white paint on the Douglas fir window frames above the sink. The difference to the room, with even this small bit of painting done, is remarkable. The room is much brighter.

Which is the major point of this exercise: *Let there be light!*

August, 2006. We step into the kitchen at 24 Armshore Drive for the first time, with our real estate agent.

"Don," I say, looking up at the one and only light in the room, "the woman does not cook." Strangely, it has turned out that Don knows the couple who are selling the house; they are not close friends, but not mere acquaintances, either.

"She may or may not," he replies, "but she is an artist – a painter – and a fine one."

"And the husband?" All the men in my family cook. But I do the cooking in my life with Don. Every meal.

"An economist."

"How do you suppose they chop anything in here?" I ask. *Aside from their fingers, off from their hands.* "Or wash dishes? It's dark as a boot." This time we both look above us to the single bulb in the centre of the room.

"I can't imagine," says Don, shaking his head.

He has shaken his head at any number of odd features to the house. But his eyes gleamed at its oceanside setting – and the mooring, small boat shop and wharf that come with the house. Mine did, too: a million-dollar setting in the city – for two writers? Can we do this? With the suite in the basement to rent out, to cover the high taxes and a small part of the mortgage, yes, Don tells me.

All the same, if we buy the house, it will take every nickel we have, with a hefty mortgage remaining. Urban waterfront does not come cheaply. We have not sold our primary residence in Cape Breton and it may take time to do this. Regardless, there will be no extra money for renovations. It is either take it, or leave it. That means old bathrooms, old appliances and the "*new* kitchen renovation, done in the 1980s." The kitchen hasn't changed much since the year it was built and Don was born: 1937.

"You know that strange light fixture in the upstairs spare bedroom?" I ask Don.

"The one with three adjustable bulbs?" He knew where I was going with this.

"Would that –"

"Yes, it would help a bit."

It did. As did the first repainting I did, which changed the plum on the pseudo-wainscoting to light yellow and added cream to the walls. I did not paint the Douglas fir trim in the room, of which there was a good deal, or the maple cabinets. I wanted time to think about what I could do, and what we could afford to have done, for further upgrades to the room. Don affixed a spotlight on a nail over the sink and with these tiny improvements, four years have passed. *There is nothing so permanent*, says a British friend of ours, *as a temporary solution that works*. And so our kitchen lighting is the same, as is the fact that our big blue house in Cape Breton has *still* not sold. Ditto the large mortgage and modest incomes.

We still can't renovate the kitchen.

And then last week we did something impulsive: we purchased a new refrigerator at the Sears Outlet Store. We had gone in to look at recliner chairs – and so, of course, left with refrigerator-lust. And why not? The new one has ... an icemaker! (Would you like cubes or crushed ice?) It's a brand-new Whirlpool! It is well-designed, so you don't have to stick most of your body into it to find a particular item, while bashing your head on the way out. It is quite the sexiest appliance in our kitchen and we can't wait for it to be delivered tomorrow.

Despite all the excitement over the fridge, the kitchen is still dark. Still hoping to change this on the cheap, I have many discussions with Denise, including ones about overall design. "I have 1930s Craftsman-style cupboards?" I repeated. "Art-deco hinges? Use William Morris-style fabric for the new curtains, to echo the '30s again? Overall, we can 'freshen' the reno done in the '80s, but can't push into the 2000s because the work would be too extensive and expensive? Decide on a 'policy plan' so we don't overspend? A colour palette, to carry with me to every store when I am purchasing kitchen items? Oh my, so much to remember!"

In the end we decide that the only cheap fix available to me is painting. And I can paint, for sure. This time the wainscoting will be white and the walls a brighter yellow. With new paint and a new white refrigerator, the kitchen will look wonderfully fresh. Can't wait!

Like the house on Armshore, the houses Don and I grew up in in Vancouver were also built in the 1930s. We both laughed when we counted up the doors in the kitchen: five. Our growing up homes both had five doors into the kitchen, too – we never expected to live with that feature again!

Don is, as we realized with great amusement early on, "the boy next door." There might have been twenty-two years of age difference between us, but we did grow up in the same city and strangely, on the same street, twenty blocks apart. Don lived at 23rd Avenue and Dunbar Street, and I lived at 43rd Avenue and Dunbar Street. I love that we know Vancouver intimately and differently, from our own decades there. We have talked endlessly about this, sharing our impressions and details of our time in the city's history. I also enjoy that we've kept up with the city and all its huge changes in the past decade, with our five overwinters there, and our many visits. There have been moments when I felt a stranger in my hometown. That has been unsettling – even unpleasant, shading on frightening. But I've pushed through those moments, did whatever observing and cataloguing I needed to do, to bring myself up to date with changes to Vancouver and its sprawling suburbs, some of which, like the historic fishing villages of Ladner and Steveston, I love as much as the city itself.

Some days I don't know who I am anymore – and most days it doesn't distress me, either. I am a Maritimer – *with all my heart* – when it suits me to be one, and I am a West Coaster from that first scent of bull kelp and the softer salt air of the Pacific Ocean.

*Oh, you are so lucky,* said a Cape Breton friend of mine once, when I told her I was sad to leave the West Coast from our latest sojourn there. *You are lucky because you are loved wherever you go, and wherever you go you love.*

Sandra Delorey is right: I am lucky.

## May 2004, Leaving Vancouver International Airport
## Planting My Flag In Cape Breton

"What did you say?" asks Don. He has swivelled in his plane seat to look at me directly in the face. He looks startled.

"I said, I can't *do* this anymore – I can't do the bi-coastal life. I just can't." My voice breaks on the last three words and I duck my face into an already soggy tissue.

"But what do you mean?" My husband takes my hand, searching frantically with his other hand for a new tissue from the outer pocket of his sports jacket. He knows the Simmins family joke about my oldest sister Zoë when she was a tiny girl, wailing to our bewildered mother: "You don't even love me enough to get me a Kleenex!", knows that I will start wailing for one any minute now. Best to be armed and ready. God knows what she'll say next, says the stricken look on his face. If Marjorie can't manage the bi-coastal life … does that mean she's leaving me and going home to B.C. again?

"I gotta plant my flag. In Cape Breton."

I stop, let that one sink in for a moment – in his mind and mine. Then: "I go to B.C., and I cry that I haven't opened up my heart enough to your life, our life, the life in C.B. I leave B.C., and I cry for my family and my friends – hell, I cry for the bridle path along the Fraser River, Nancy's pony barn, my favourite thrift stores – the goddamned endless rain! These visits out West – we don't really live here, as in living our lives. It's only pretend-time. Suspended time. The place you stand in when you're waiting to go home to Cape Breton. And the hardest thing of all, the part I really can't take in on a gut level? I can't make you love it. I was so sure I could. Not just love it – but re-love it. You were brought up here! We even lived in the same neighbourhood – we grew up, exactly twenty blocks apart. You know this place – in some ways better than I do, from earlier years."

I shake my head, tears darkening the shiny grey cloth of my seatbelt. "I even thought maybe you'd forgotten, that once you spent some time out here again ... well, you'd meet up with me and share all that big love of place. Instead you only endure the West Coast until we're home again in the Maritimes."

"Come on, I don't just endure it – I love seeing my family and old friends, too, you know that. Your family and friends now, too. And the city is pleasant enough. But no, you can't make me love Vancouver. I never did."

*I never did* – and never will, no matter what I do or say. The plane walls feel like they are pushing in. I look out the window, searching to "sight" an horizon, as though I am seasick. We're still on the tarmac, the plane nose facing the airport buildings. No horizon to be seen.

I know this resonant moment well; sometimes it seems like the surrounding landscape of my life. It is the Place Of No Compromise. I find the love of my life ... and we make our life together four thousand miles away from everything cherished and familiar to me – a land with no cherry blossoms, and a spring so short and violent that some years, you go from winter clothes to bathing suits in under two weeks. Vancouver's spring takes a lazy fragrant flower-bedazzled four months to unfold.

The tissue, located finally in an inside pocket, appears in Don's right hand. It is crumpled but clean. He proffers it.

"Thank you." I smile wanly, understanding how my sister felt: no Kleenex, no love. Who wants to have a meltdown and be distracted by a dripping nose?

And my God, I am distracted. We've been living the bi-coastal life for five years now. We leave the East Coast in the frigid white winter and arrive, ten hours later, in a temperate green place where snowdrops rise in February. We've had a spring in Gibsons, on the Sunshine Coast, two springs in Point Roberts, Washington, one in Richmond and one in Steveston; actually living in Vancouver would be impossibly expensive. We pack up four months' worth of clothes and endless banker's boxes full of work files, reference books, office supplies. We pack up the dog. Out comes the travel crate and in goes Leo, all on his own: *Don't forget your whippet*, say Don and I jokingly to one another. Leo's maple-syrup-coloured eyes are indeed sweet but long-suffering, too. It is torture for me to hear his disconsolate cries as the baggage crew pull up in their small truck and cart, alongside the plane: *yip! yip! yeee-ip!* Such a cold trip for our short-haired hound, despite his fleecy coat. Deafening, too. On top of everything else, I feel like A Heartless Dog Owner. Leo never asked for all this moving around and confusion. All he ever wants is to be with us. What a price.

"No more," I say. "Not fair to you, not fair to Leo."

"Not good for you, either," says Don. "And in truth, hard to sustain financially."

I know. I know all these things. Guilt. Fatigue. Longing. Grief. And suddenly I have to breathe through my mouth to gulp in enough air to float my heart upward, from the far place it's fallen.

*"I'd say to the man, good luck getting my sister out of B.C.,"* said Geoffrey, all those years ago now. I look over to Don, see the warm concerned eyes of the man I love and say what I need to say, what I know I must say, to bring peace and balance back to our lives: "Let's go home."

# 21

## HOMELANDS

Homelands. I am so lucky, to have so many. For me, a homeland is a place of comfort and belonging; it can be a river, shoreline or barn, a boat, person or dog. It can be a personal pathway of thought or intellectual sharings. It can be a scent. Homelands can circulate in our blood, too, remind us of other times and places. These can be our own histories that we have forgotten – or these can be the histories that only our forebears knew, but tucked away in the shadows between our bones and flesh.

A letter arrives from my younger sister Jessica. I read it at my desk at my home in Halifax.

She's going back to playing the bagpipe, and she's excited.

I look away from the colourful card in my hands, smiling. I smile because I am happy to know Jessica wants to return to regular music practice and I smile broader thinking about her re-chosen instrument, which is not everyone's ... first choice for musical pleasure.

*Ah, the bagpipes ... a homeland of the blood that called out to a tiny girl, newly arrived on the West Coast of Canada from Ottawa, Ontario.*

## Vancouver, British Columbia, 1963

The Vancouver Art Gallery's long cement balcony is on the second floor, thirty feet up from Georgia Street. Today it is filled with V.I.P., my parents tell me. That would be friends, family and favoured artists of the gallery's director, my father, Richard Simmins, or "Tim," as my mother sometimes calls him in fond moods. Traffic was heavy an hour ago. Now the street itself is empty, though behind the barricades people form thick fringes on either side of it. Laughter and rapid words rise. People on the balcony are chattering, too. The city parade is about to begin.

It is hot and I squirm in my mother's arms. I am not tall enough to see over the balcony's edge; I only turned four in February. It is May now. We've only been here in Vancouver for a few weeks. It is a big green salt-aired city. I love it when we go for drives around Stanley Park, see the immense, bark-rippled Douglas fir and clusters of totem poles. I also love my dad's gallery, which he fills with colourful art and objects – "putting on shows," that's what directors do. Some of the art has moving wheels and buttons to push and makes all sorts of noises. Art doesn't always mean a painting with a frame, says Dad, impatiently at times. Sometimes you can even touch the art in his gallery. There are cards placed right beside them that say you can. But don't ever touch the paintings, like all the green swirling ones by Emily Carr. Dad scowls if you try to do that.

I squirm again, impatient for more than just the tops of heads to look down on. Then, without warning, a single throbbing wail fills the air, flanked immediately by other wails, all strengthening. It could be fifty doors creaking open all at once. Instantly my arms begin to sting; tiny bees poke their way along them from shoulder to wrist, even into my fingertips. Every arm-hair is erect, vibrates in a world now filled only with this sharp scraping keening. My head swivels right, towards the North Shore mountains. I see a long line of kilted men growing bigger with each stride. I see the red plaid of their kilts, white knee-socks, dark jackets with gold braid on the cuffs – and strange, tilted hats on the men's heads. The hats are like blocky wigs with long black tufts of fabric-hair. The men march in a unison so precise it makes me clench my fists in envy: to be *one of many, many of one* – I want this fiercely, for no reasons I can pin onto anything, and for all reasons, I will come to know, related to Irish and Scottish blood and heritage. My teeth bite against my lower lip, and if I blinked, tears would spill. I do not blink, only stare fixedly. The drums are already aligned with my heartbeats. But what are those awkward shapes with spokes that some of the men are carrying against their shoulders?

*Bagpipes,* my mother whispers into my ear, aware of the questions humming in my rigid body, *and the song they're playing is "Scotland the Brave."* With fists still shut tight a tapping of words crosses my mind: *One of many many of one – one two one two one two* … There, I've steadied my heartbeat, perhaps I can be brave, too. The music is fading, though the parade has only just started. My mother puts me on my feet, asks if I'd like something to drink. It's even hotter now and I am thirsty so I nod yes. We excuse ourselves through the crowd on the balcony, go in search of water. As we walk I think about that word, *brave,* and I decide I am not really sure what it means. Maybe it means marching like the pipers and drummers, one step after another, not stopping when you're hot and thirsty, confused, maybe, by an earth and sky of sound all around you and nowhere to slip away to, where the quiet lives and a heartbeat can steady. Or maybe brave means holding back the tears, when life makes bee stings on your arms.

* * *

I am still not sure what being brave is – maybe the meanings for that change over a lifetime, too. Mostly I think being brave is showing up with verve and humour for your life, seizing and sharing all the goodness and experiences therein. And when you are scared? I mean really heart-hurts frightened? Jump anyway. But land with your knees bent, arms up, if you can. Remember your lion-tamer mother's blood flows in your veins, along with the father-blood of a man who fought in a world war when he was seventeen.

Music was *such* a help, to ground me in feelings of home when I moved to Nova Scotia. My father was right – I was far more Canadian than Celtic – but for all that, I believe hereditary memory is real. (The first time I smelled pungent burning peat, in the fireplace of an Irish pub, I stopped as though slapped and could only think, "I know this.") Attitude and interests also aided my transition. My heart was – to use a Cape Breton expression – "wide open" to the Celtic music of the Atlantic region, even before my first trip there. The Rankin Family may have grown up in Mabou, Cape Breton, but their rollicking songs with their soaring harmonies had travelled across Canada and well beyond. I mean, didn't everyone in the world want to hit that shattering high note that the late and cherished Raylene Rankin did at the end of "We Rise Again"? Even I, an enthusiastic but untrained alto, tried it on for size. And I may not have known where Orangedale was, but I loved the joyous "Orangedale Whistle," too, and thought it had to be a memorable place to be thought worthy of capturing in song (*yes*). There were many East Coast folk and Celtic musicians whose names and music I knew well while I was still a Vancouverite, among them Stan Rogers, Ashley MacIsaac, Rita MacNeil and Natalie MacMaster. Again pre-Cape Breton, Don was quick to mail me CDs of younger Celtic bands, such as the Barra MacNeils, and other established geniuses such as Scott Macmillan and John Allan Cameron. I thought Don was teasing when he said he knew some of these people as friends. He wasn't. He'd even travelled to China and sung with Men of the Deeps, an all-male choir of former Cape Breton coal miners, in the 1970s.

For me, and us, right then though, it was the mid-1990s. I am ready, I thought, preparing for that first trip to Cape Breton. Bring on the music, and bring on the fiddlers and pipers. And bring it on, Don did, with relish. One summer we watched over two hundred fiddlers perform on an outdoor stage at the Gaelic College in St. Ann's, Cape Breton. Every autumn we attended The Celtic Colours International Festival, held in community venues across Cape Breton

Island, featuring modern and traditional Celtic music performed by Canadian stars and musicians from around the world. Another time we saw a new young Celtic fusion band called Slainte Mhath (*slawncha va*), which featured the rockin'-est Highland bagpipes and Scottish smallpipes we'd either of us ever heard. Our eardrums did backflips just to match the movement of sound. No bee stings when I heard this band, but I did wish I could paint my face blue and let loose a Highlander war whoop. Years later the bees returned, even swarmed me, when the bagpipes were played at the funeral of a beloved friend of ours from Grand Anse, Sharon Urquhart. Dressed in the MacInnis tartan, her handsome cousin Rod MacInnis piped her on to another home – though fiercely was she loved in this sphere, and fiercely is she still missed. Music is very much used to honour people in the Maritimes.

The music of Cape Breton Island is almost impossible to summarize or pay full credit to: it's in the seeds of the meadow grass and in every shoreward-tumbling Atlantic Ocean or Bras d'Or Lakes' wave. It is also dependably prolific. Of the unusual number of spectacularly gifted fiddlers raised on the island and set loose on the world, old-timers have been known to say, smiling, "It's in the water." Specifically, they mean the water along Route 19, the west coast of the island, which winds its way along the high rocky coast overlooking the Gulf of St. Lawrence through Judique and up along to Inverness, then darts inland to the music-mad villages of Mabou and Margaree Harbour. Name *any* village on Cape Breton Island and you will likely find someone "playing tunes": in the community centre, church hall, living rooms, barns or on the wharves or front porches. It is how people live with each other in Cape Breton and in Atlantic Canada – especially during the long winters. And while I believe it is fair to call the violin or "fiddle" king in these places, there are also the crown princes and princesses of piano, guitar, mandolin, bodhrán, accordion and Irish flute.

Jessica, like our brother Geoffrey, picks up languages and music with ease and enthusiasm. I don't have the inborn facility they do, but I have had, periodically, the stubbornness to jog short distances alongside the truly fluent and musically gifted. My French, therefore, could be used to save my own life or someone else's (*j'espère*), and to locate bathrooms, good restaurants and of course, *les bureaux de poste, pour mes lettres.*

As for music, I can easily resurrect the folk-music past I shared with my brother, accompanying myself singing on my ancient (1974) but still resonant twelve-string Yamaki Deluxe guitar and new Baby Taylor. This I did, for some years in Cape Breton, happily adding favourite anthems of the region. I cannot, absolutely cannot, sing through "Song for the Mira" without my voice breaking on its wrenching lyrics about arriving broken – and becoming mended, by the love of the people of the region. *Don was broken when he arrived in 1971 – divorced and missing his four children terribly – and mended. I was broken when I first visited, in 1996, and I mended, too.*

Nor can I sing through "Heading for Halifax" – even though I did head for Halifax and stayed there. It's that leaving the heart behind part of the song that makes my own heart a pretzel; loss, and the fear of it, these are central themes in everyone's life. But in Cape Breton it's not just the people you love who you are leaving behind. It's also the heart-catching geography. You never travel away from Cape Breton without feeling the power of its ancient rugged hills trying to pull you back. I feel the same way walking or riding a horse along the banks of the Fraser River. As though any other homeland would lack the majesty to keep you ever-near, contented. Why would you ever want to leave? And yet you must, to take on new challenges and experiences – to grow and develop professionally and personally.

There is no homeland more consistent and elemental to my happiness than the company of the man I married. Don understands ... *everything* – my sprints and tumbles through this world, my great loves and fears, my humming head, my dreams and needs, and my ability to worry and self-criticize. He even understands, bless him always, the Simmins' famously *non sequitur* communications.

"Of course I haven't heard from her in weeks," I say out of the clear blue, seated at the kitchen table and not long after a query for the milk to put on my cereal. "No," he responds immediately, courteously passing me the milk first and then adding: "But then, it is summer, Mary Jane could be on vacation with her family." This is Don-speak for Don't worry, all is well, and even if it isn't, all is manageable – one way or another, at one time or another.

Once in a great long while he somehow doesn't follow .the byzantine connections to a thought I've voiced. He laughs or shakes his head or puts both palms up – *I surrender* – or all three. "How did you get from there to – ?" He laughs a lot harder when I explain the relentless and peculiar travellings of my thoughts, though doesn't quite concede these might be *logical* to an audience larger than the two assembled. "Nonsense," I say briskly, addressing his unvoiced thought, "it makes perfect sense if you're paying attention" – all of which really is nonsense, which I know and he knows and just makes us start yet another blessed day of our life together with laughter.

There is one other homeland with Don that I cherish at a deep level every day. We are writers. We met as writers, grew as writers, continue to change and grow as writers – and we live in this world each and every day as writers. What does that mean? It means we have big ears and fall in love with the dialogue and stories we hear around us. It can mean we go a bit fuzzy around the edges when said dialogue is occurring; the pen to paper that is our minds is writing furiously, taking down the notes that we can develop later on, seated at our separate desks. We talk about words – a lot. We read – more. We share our findings – in conversation and in e-mails. Don often recites poetry; his sticky mind has memorized dozens of poems, short and long, classic and modern. I attach song lyrics to my days or moods; there are always some that fit, just *so,* hummed or only thought about. We share our own writings with one another on a near-daily basis; an e-mail here (social plannings/catch-up notes when we're apart), a business letter there (future work), articles, book chapters. Does it work? we ask sometimes. Or, could you please proofread this? Or – the dreaded – did I miss something important?

The best reaction of all? Tears. Hard to say who would be more delighted to make the other person cry with a piece of writing: *gotcha, my words gotcha!* Probably me. When I hear that gentle tread coming down from the office upstairs to mine on the first floor of our Halifax house, and look around to see Don holding a printout of my work, his eyes brimming – 'tis a black-heartedly enjoyable moment. Of which we will never tire.

## 22

## ANNIVERSARY

### MARCH 14, 2011, HALIFAX, NOVA SCOTIA

Thirteen years ago today ... It was a grand wedding ... it is a grand life ...

Today has been a regular workday around here, but tonight we are going out to one of the best restaurants in the city, Fiasco. There will be no Weight Watchers' fixation tonight! We have both lost fifteen pounds since October 2 and are feeling very happy about that. Don is almost at his "goal weight." I have another fifteen pounds to go, I hope. But no calorie counting tonight. Only pure debauched pleasure. Bring it on!

On this special anniversary day I had a special e-mail from my riding instructor, Heidi, to make my mood even lighter.

"Hi Marjorie, 10:00 on Wednesday for a lesson sounds great – I will see you then. Yes, you are looking much stronger in the tack and now that it is spring you may have the bug to ride a little more so you will notice big improvements. See you soon. Thanks, Heidi"

... *much stronger in the tack* ... an unusual phrasing, one I've never heard before – but I'll take it!

It was actually a great ride, that last one on Friday morning. I felt like me, a real rider again. Buddy was a bit of a pain when I was tacking him up – my God, he must have had people hauling on that girth over the years to make him so nippy, crabby and ready to kick with hind *and* forelegs! – but good as gold under saddle. My ankles felt stronger, my back, arms and calves felt stronger, I had "weight" in my heels, decent posture and soft hands. As I say, real. Buddy the Quarter horse, unsurprisingly, has a lovely lope and better yet, doesn't fade out on the corners. Often used to work cattle on ranches or for "Western Pleasure" riding classes at horse shows (among many other activities), the average Quarter horse is muscular, has a dependable work ethic – and is sizzling fast, to keep up with sprinting calves that run off from the herd. These horses need to be comfortable for their cowboy/girl riders, who can spend many hours in the saddle. Even though Buddy has been trained for English-style riding, the genes remain. I think he could canter right off the edge of the horizon with no particular help from my modest leg muscles.

Despite his grumpy ways, I am getting fond of old Buddy. And he is old, too. Heidi says he's twenty-two, and his back end isn't always the steadiest. He slipped under himself several times on Friday, which gave my neck some good jerks in the process and really hurt. I don't think his slips were caused by the footing in the indoor arena, which was not too deep and nicely raked. I must mention this to Heidi. If it's arthritis, as I suspect it may be, there's nothing she can do about it, but she should know and keep an eye on him for soundness. Ah, old horses – they give and give until there's only the essence of ability left.

Time to put on a party dress. Heels, too! Red.

## MARCH 15, 2011, HALIFAX, NOVA SCOTIA

Fiasco was wonderful. Taxi dismissed, in from the frigid winter world we came, to a restaurant where candles added star-points to a ruby-walled room. Velvet curtains and white linens softened the sound of our footsteps, muted other patrons' voices. Bold abstract art encircled the walls. Model-beautiful young women inquired, Had we been to Fiasco before? then settled us at the mahogany bar, at the end of which was set a heavy crystal vase, filled with fragrant, pink Asian lilies.

The martinis we started the evening with were pastel-pretty, diabolically thirst-quenching and exhilarating. We sipped them, studied the menu, made our choices for supper. In time, we moved to our reserved window table to eat our meals.

There is a certain mathematical precision to the taste of superbly prepared food. The numbers all add up. There are no mistakes in the additions or subtractions. If there is to be a blend of sweet and sour, then the blend is perfect. If the dish calls for garlic, mango and chili, then this blend, too, is just right. First came the calamari, which presented as the happiest marriage of Italian and Szechuan – two of the finest cuisines in the world, for my tastes. Then came halibut, prawns and scallops, arriving in different sauces in different guises of appetizer and main courses. All were thirty seconds underdone, for maximum flavour. Our Italian sparkling rose was dry, with a base note of smoky fruit. No, no, thank you, we wouldn't have dessert – and yet dessert "came with the meal," and so we agreed to try one spoonful of the passionfruit and white chocolate ice cream. Mischievous fairies, darting out from behind the velvet curtains, ate the rest of the ice cream, which melted faster than snow in fog.

Don was handsome, dressed in a new charcoal sports jacket, white shirt, tie and sky-blue fine wool vest. He was also relaxed and affectionate. I wanted to wear a dress – but could not face the notion of nylons on such a cold night, and so wore a black ensemble that, if not as feminine as I wanted, was at least smart and slimming. I punctuated the black with red high heels and a red scarf. My mood was as light as Don's. We don't go out for these thoroughly extravagant evenings very often.

The only problem was the shock to our Weight Watchers' stomachs, which could barely manage the number of courses and the emphatic richness of all the food. We enjoyed ourselves. But won't be repeating the experience any time soon!

Minus ten this morning. Spring recedes from reality yet again. I was going to check for snowdrops in the backyard yesterday – never did, too cold for garden investigations. But flowers can't come up in this cold, anyway. Need to turn off the Vancouver part of my brain, which hungers to see colour, smell garden growth, from March onward.

"Two more months of winter yet to go, Marjorie," said Denise cheerfully yesterday. "May as well get used to it." I won't tell her that last weekend's plus-ten temperatures made me pack up my heavier sweaters and down coats to be stored in the attic. I brought them down again earlier this week. Flowers, spring clothes – I am trying to be patient and it's not working this year.

At least I have the colour of daffodils in my kitchen now. One more blessed door to paint, and I am done. New flooring will have to wait for more funds, as will the addition of some new cupboards, a stove fan and microwave. What I have done has made a huge difference, though. The room is bright and so much easier to work in now. Makes me happy. Makes me, oddly, want to "celebrate," have a cigarette. Will that thought-linkage ever go away: celebrate=cigarette? Cigarettes were never the "treats" we committed smokers viewed them to be – only little death-sticks, shortening our lives with each inhalation. I still miss them, still fight the urge to smoke some days. But less and less often, thank goodness. And more and more often, I am deeply happy to be a non-smoker.

It's been more than ten years since Don quit. For me, it's been eight years, three months and fifteen days.

Or thereabouts.

## GOODBYE TO CIGARETTES
### D'ESCOUSSE, NOVA SCOTIA, 2003

"Can you hand me up the other curtain?" My husband is standing precariously on top of my desk, which is actually two doors laid out in an L-configuration, supported at the ends by file cabinets, and in the middle by a wooden frame of sorts. Under his left arm, he holds one-half of a curtain rod, onto which the first freshly laundered cotton panel has been slid; in his right hand, the other half of the rod, waiting for its mate. I am too short to manage this bit of housekeeping on my own. Apart from that, I am also far too frayed for any task requiring manual dexterity. I'll be lucky if I can remember where to place my feet to walk. *How could I have forgotten how hard this is?*

It's day nine of quitting cigarettes. Only five short months since my last try at quitting and yet until now I've managed to forget how violent the cravings for cigarettes can be. My desire to smoke is all-encompassing and amoral. I would lie, cheat, steal – fill in the blank however shockingly you please – to haul in a full, long drag of myriad poisons, tar and nicotine. At the very least, I would happily play in heavy traffic to nab just one narrow cylinder filled with tobacco. I retain only the merest shreds of integrity: I will not barter away husband, hound or house for a tailor-made cigarette. I think.

"I thought these curtains were yellow," says my innocent husband quizzically. He tugs together the two dazzling white panels, to block out the sun-glare on my computer screen so I can work.

"They were," I sigh. "Nicotine stains. I bleached them."

"Oh," comes the wondering reply. "That's hard to believe."

No harder to believe than crashing and burning – after eighty smoke-free days this spring. The cause? Some self-generated life drama, which at the time seemed overwhelming. A friend of mine had dared to live her own life, complete with making her own decisions, which left me feeling betrayed and marginalized. Actions thus (conveniently) rationalized, I fell on a pouch of tobacco like a hungry terrier on a rat. Cigarettes raise the blood pressure, say all the experts. And yet on that day back in April, I clearly remember how effective the first inhalation of tobacco was: instant relief, of the heavily tranquillizing sort. I was not happy – cognitively – to experience that. I was, in fact, appalled. Beyond this, however, I was forced to make a crucial admission deep within my psyche.

I retain no illusions about my addiction: I am powerless over it, and need all the help I can get to remain cigarette-free.

"How's the patch feel today?" asks my husband. He is poised at the door of my office, would like, I know, to get on with his own workday. But he never stints on his support during this difficult time for me.

"Good, as always." I'd forgotten how strong the Nicoderm patch is – the patch itself almost "burns" my skin, and makes the surrounding muscle area ache heavily – but I am once again glad for its calming effects. Unlike the last time – does the ante go up with each quitting attempt? – I am also using Nicorette gum, which I find very effective in combating sudden, severe cravings. My jaw, too, aches by the end of each day.

"And when's your first class?"

Cigarette school. More officially, the Dr. W. B. Kingston Memorial Clinic Health Project – whew! What a mouthful! – I attended before, which is again offering sessions for those wanting to quit cigarettes.

"A week from now." The program runs for ten weeks, each Monday night, at a high school in St. Peter's. I need to hear the laughter, feel the camaraderie of those Cig School sessions again. Free-range babble and sharing, and informative, non-judgemental professionals guiding the sessions. Walk tall, everyone fails at some things, not everyone tries again. One day at a time, as the twelve-step programs advise. On goes the internal chatter, as I stare, shoulders slumped, at my blank computer screen.

"So there's nothing else you ... ?" I turn to see him spread out his hands in a helpless gesture.

I shake my head, attempt a smile. No, nothing else I need. Only a new, non-addicted brain. Perhaps a new life history, one from which my thirty-year dependence on tobacco is deleted. While you're at it, throw in some new lungs and a lottery win to cover all the money I've wasted on this stupid – *oh please, all I want is one little puff* –

Stop. Now. Must think about something positive, something significant and life-enhancing about the cig-free life.

I pick up a pen and start doodling on a small notepad. I'll make a list, see if that helps. I'll start with the very best feature of quitting last time. Uh, that would be ...

The facelift. That would be number one. It wasn't a real one, of course, that would be too scary, but as physical changes go, the difference to my post-cigarette facial skin was amazing. I could finally understand the cliché roses in her cheeks. I had those roses, for the first time since I was a teenager. There wasn't a mirror in the world I didn't pause in front of, to shamelessly stare at my new face.

"You look so pretty!" said my husband day after day. Yeah, I could stand to have that scenario again. No appreciable change at this point. But soon, I hope. If vanity can help me stay resolute, so be it.

Number two, decent callouses on my fingertips. The blues are so much a part of quitting cigarettes that playing the blues on my guitar just seemed like a natural thing to do. I may have been "hurtin'" from the withdrawal process, but for once, my fingertips were not complaining. That was a treat, to play as much as I wanted, with no need to snivel about tender digits. Name of the game: hands busy, mind distracted.

Three, I had breath to sing. Breath to enjoy walking more. Breath that could be taken in deeply, with no shadings of obstruction, deep in my chest. Those had frightened me, as well they should.

Four, perspective and optimism. The two went hand in hand – and cannot, when I am smoking. You can't have perspective on an addiction overcome, and feel cheery about that, when you're still indulging. With only three months cig-sober, I am nowhere near to a full understanding of why I would tolerate self-destructive behaviour in myself. There is no need for this. Nor were there enough days of freedom to bask in feelings of accomplishment. Only the briefest period to realize there are quieter ways to pass through this life. Smokers are coiled springs, the chemicals they inhale keeping them forever in the state of flight or fight. I don't wish to live that way anymore.

"Just use your willpower," said a well-meaning friend lately, "and you'll be fine."

It's not quite that simple. When the occasional waft of tobacco comes to me when I am out and about in the wider world, it feels like a spike of desire slamming through my brain. Run, girl, run. See the girl run. Physically, I can remove myself from negative situations. Emotionally, the movements are more hesitant. This battle will be won in the realm of spirit, I believe. And pray.

I turn back to my computer screen, determined to finally start my workday. And yet as I begin typing I hear the rueful voice of another friend who quit cigarettes for four months this year, and then started again: "Never say never!" All right, I won't. But for today, I haven't smoked. And that brings a measure of contentment.

Click, click, click, the first line comes to me: "Can you hand me up that other curtain?"

## 23

## THINGS ARE NOT ALWAYS AS THEY SEEM

### MARCH 24, 2011, 10:00 A.M., HALIFAX, NOVA SCOTIA

Don is away in Cape Breton. He has two speaking engagements and we also needed to check on our two houses in D'Escousse. Houses do not like being left unpeopled, especially over the course of a Nova Scotian winter. The large blue house, our former primary residence, has been for sale since 2006; it is empty, pipes drained, heat off. The smaller "Morrison House," which we hope to keep as a Cape Breton summer home, is across the road from the blue house in the centre of the village; it is furnished, functional and heated. Even still, Don decided not to stay at the Morrison House this time round. Instead he is staying, by invitation of his brother-in-law, at his home, also located in D'Escousse.

Brother-in-law. No, this is not my brother, Geoffrey, though he is Don's brother-in-law, no question, as is my older sister Zoë's husband, Garney, and younger (half-) sister Jessica's husband, Mark. The brother-in-law he is staying with is one of Lulu's brothers, with whom he has a strong friendship, though he remains in contact with all of Lulu's siblings and gets on well with all of them, too. He is close to some of their children, also; these young men and women call him "Uncle Don," which he is, ever and always, through marriage to Lulu.

*Marriage to Lulu* – it is a phrase I've heard a lot over the years. The marriage remains as real now, in some ways, as it did for the seventeen years they spent as husband and wife, from 1979 to 1996. Don still calls Lulu's mother "Mum," and Lulu's sisters and brothers remain his sisters-in-law and brothers-in-law. Lulu's son Mark, fathered by her Danish first husband, is still – of course – Don's legally adopted son. For all those who knew her, liked her or loved her, Lulu's death was *only a new way of living with her*. From the beginning, I couldn't help but see similarities in the death of my sister Karin, one of four (full) siblings, and the death of Lulu, one of ten siblings. I and sometimes my sisters and brother still talk about Karin. Don, Mark, Lulu's nine siblings, Lulu's mother Mimi, and occasionally some of Lulu's friends and neighbours, still talk about Lulu. Karin has been, to some degree, demonized; it's easier to live with her early death that way. Lulu has been, to some degree, beatified; it's easier to live with her early death that way. Why should I not talk about someone I loved and lost? Why shouldn't the Terrio family talk about a member of their tribe who they loved and lost? Don't we all have the photographs, keepsakes, memories – and for some of us, the nightmares – to prove the dead once lived among us?

I dreamed about Lulu – once and once only. The dream frightened me so badly I didn't know how to live with the memory. Every time the memory recurred – on little cat feet, a cold fog all of its own. – I'd have to jump up and walk it away. This I did out of the blue house, out, strangely, on the beaches Lulu had walked herself – Pondville, The Tiddle, Martinique Park – but unlike Lulu, I walked with my dog, Leo. His gentle, contented soul calmed my shaken one – every time. The calming would not happen quickly, though. Before it did, I would rage at Lulu, calling her down, impossibly, from a fair sky to fight fair, too, on that beach, in that moment, eye to eye and woman to woman. Yes, I knew it was her husband, house, boat, region, island, family and life I'd inherited – her own mother called me her "daughter's successor" – but goddamn it, wasn't I alive and she dead? Didn't that fundamental difference count for anything? Wasn't that sure knowledge of breath in my lungs supposed to make me feel empowered – stronger, at least, than even the most vividly remembered shade of a woman? It's taken a decade to realize, yet again, *that things are not always as they seem.*

## THE BASEMENT DREAM

The wooden stairs to the basement are narrow and twisting. I am mid-staircase, just before the stairs take a sharp left, continue down – one, two, three, four – to the cement-floored space. It's dark. I am having trouble seeing. I have paused because the rises are steep for me and suddenly, I don't know where to place my feet. It would be so easy to trip, break a leg or an arm, even a neck. I am going to the basement to get something from the freezer for supper. I don't remember what is in the freezer. Perhaps I don't really have a freezer. Perhaps there is only cold emptiness here.

Something is holding my foot. Something is holding my ankle. Someone is muttering, voice coming from the stair beneath my feet. It's still dark and it's still cold and now I can't move that right leg at all. I can move the other foot – but then suddenly, I can't. It's as though both feet are glued to the stair. I am having trouble breathing. I can still move my arms and I swat those about. I hit the wood on either side of the staircase. It is soft, as though I have hit a body. A groan rumbles from under the stair. I drop my hands to my sides again. I am aware of pain, but I don't know whose pain it is – the flesh-walls I just hit, or my own lungs, out of which air is being pushed by the heavy darkness all around me. Fear is icicles frigid against my flesh, the tips seeking entry under the skin as a needle seeks to imbed thread. Perhaps I will be sewn to the flesh-walls, left there in the dark to breathe in tandem with the groaning undead. I feel electrically alive and consumed with will. I need to turn around somehow, climb back up the stairs. I must free my feet. I will free my feet.

*Do you think you are that strong?* Lulu. The words are not spoken aloud. But I hear them in each cell of my body.

*Yes, yes I am that strong.* These words, too, have no sound. But they smash against the flesh-walls suddenly made wood again: *bang bang bang.* Take that.

The grip on my feet loosens – this may not last. I think myself up several stairs; my body still isn't moving freely. *Let me go.*

*No. Not yet.*

One leg is free, the other held with a weakening hand. With my two free arms I drag myself up the last two stairs. I lie in a slanted pool of light, on a blond wood floor – on the other, closed side of the door to the basement.

It's as though I've swallowed the voice from below. *Go then,* I hear her say, as close as my own heartbeat. *Go.*

How could I go? I had just come to live there. I thought I'd have to live with her angry presence. I didn't understand, couldn't understand, then, that she wasn't angry at all. She was trying to protect me. To make me listen.

# 24

## RETROSPECT, CAPE BRETON

### MARCH 28, 2011, HALIFAX, NOVA SCOTIA

The wind has been relentless here in Halifax this winter. The way it was so often in Cape Breton – and that could be in any season. I'd never felt a house sway in the winds before I lived in D'Escousse. And that's a solid, well-built house. The house Don bought in the late '70s may have been in near to ruinous shape, but its "bones" or beams and joists were formidable, irreplaceable in today's Maritime wood market. The Victorian-style house was first built in the late nineteenth century. When Don and Lulu renovated it in the 1980s, they decided to keep all of its classic features such as its original design of two offset rectangles, the ten-foot ceilings and the exterior "gingerbread" or elaborate "knees" of carved wood decorations on the roof corners. Inside, they gutted the house. The main floor was beautifully redone, with a modern IKEA kitchen, a fireplace that faced two rooms and hardwood floors throughout. The upstairs ... didn't quite get finished ...

## MAY 1998

"Are you happy, dear? Are you really happy?" Dad always sounds a bit worried when he calls me these days. Oddly, now that I have moved four thousand miles from B.C. to Cape Breton, I am now geographically closer to my once again Ontario-based father than I have been most of my life. My dad's fragile heart-health prevented his presence at our wedding in March; the trip out west from Ontario was just too onerous. After Don and I married, and I relocated to Cape Breton, Dad has continued to do as he has done since my early twenties: he writes and phones me weekly. He is concerned about my move from a big city I love to a country village of 250 residents, and as concerned about my writerly transition to the region. He also knows how devoted I have been to my West Coast girlfriends all my life – "Your friends," says my sister Zoë, "they've always been your kids" – and my long-standing connection to the horse world in Vancouver. I am on my own here. Thank God for my whippet Leo, and my new friends, Denise, Murielle and Ann.

"Papa," I say, smiles all over my voice, "don't worry, I'm fine." I tell him about my latest house projects – this week I am painting the porcelain claw-foot tub in our ensuite bathroom – forest-green tub, gold "toes" – while recovering from last week's job of reglazing the interior. I actually wore a professional painter's mask when I did the reglazing. It made no difference. I was high as a Georgia pine for forty-eight hours, and couldn't slug back enough water to rehydrate. Never again. But the tub looks brand new.

"I got the photos," laughs Dad. "They're great!" Don had taken photos of me dressed in a white Kevlar jumpsuit, the painter's mask tight on my face, a paintbrush in hand – this is the second tub I have refinished on the second floor; the other one is royal blue with gold toes – and I had sent them along to Dad in recent letters. My father, in his latest life incarnation, is a photographer. He tells me to document my life visually, and I am doing this. After twenty-five years, I no longer write a daily journal. I still write letters, six or seven a week, but there is no time left over for the journal. Photos seem easier at this point. I also like having a record of the changes to the upstairs and around the house and gardens generally. I've been working hard.

\* \* \*

"How do I clean the bathroom floors?" I asked Don when I looked at the chipboard on the two bathroom floors upstairs in 1997, the first year I lived with Don in D'Escousse. How did one swab chipboard?

"Number one, you don't clean them," he answered. "Ruth does. Number two, she uses a cloth mop."

Right, Ruth, Lulu's best friend in D'Escousse. She cleaned the house for Don and Lulu for years, cared devotedly for Lulu until she died, and still housecleaned for Don. For us. I had no clue how to deal with this. I'd never had someone scrub my toilets before. I reverted to being my mother's child, and tried to make sure things were nice and clean before Ruth arrived each Saturday. *Cleaning for the cleaning woman, as the expression goes.* (Ruth's warmth and kindness to me was immediate and constant. This generosity floored me and, conversely, made me anxious: in the same circumstances, could I ever be this accepting of life's strange and painful twists?)

"You are missing the point – entirely," said Don. "I am trying to buy you time to write." I understood. But I was really uncomfortable with this whole set-up, which had been in place for some time.

"Ruth started helping us when Mark went to school and Lulu went back to work," said Don. He explained that Lulu started doing renovations on the island and loved the work more than any other work she'd done. Don still owned and rented out all the houses they had renovated. I could barely keep them and the constant in-and-out flow of tenants straight. People came from Isle Madame ... and people went, mostly out west to Fort McMurray.

"Too many houses," I grumbled. They sucked up a lot of Don's time. Renovations only serve so long. Maintenance and repairs are a constant, as are whingeing and often insolvent tenants.

Don was unfailingly pleasant and creatively helpful to his tenants; a "come-from-away," he was permanently grateful to have been accepted into the Isle Madame community, and he didn't care if a rent cheque took months to be paid, as long as it was paid eventually. Many never did pay, and as often left a damaged or filthy apartment behind them. Don took it all in stride.

"I ran up credit myself at Pearl's for years," he told me, referring to the small general store owned by Ray and Pearl LeBlanc in D'Escousse. His freelance income was small and erratic in those early years on Isle Madame; he was also heartsick, slowly reshaping his life after his divorce from his first wife, Ann Cameron, who remained in their marital home in Fredericton, with their four children.

In his early years in D'Escousse, Don was establishing himself as a freelance writer and author. He made little money. He doesn't forget the kindnesses shown to him by the community.

"Ray and Pearl LeBlanc didn't care how long I ran a tab; they ran tabs for all kinds of people who needed help. That's what this place is all about, helping people when they're down and being happy we live in this great place." Don's voice is resonant and proud; you'd think he'd fathered Isle Madame as a concept and reality, all on his own.

"Houses," I said teasingly, doing some circling back of my own. "How many houses do you own at this point?"

"Oh, a few," Don said airily. "Do you remember their names?"

"Sure. There's the Morrison House, the Joyce House, Charlie's House and Telile."

Telile was easy to remember. It was the commercial building across the island to the south from D'Escousse, in the village of Arichat. The building had four apartments and a main-floor commercial space for Télévision Isle Madame, or TELILE, the community television company that Don, Lulu and many others on Isle Madame had begun in the early 1990s.

"You forgot one." Damn, he's right. It's hardly a house – more like a demolition zone. It's not in our village, either, but just up the road to the east, in the village of Poirierville –

"The Mauger House."

"Are you really serious about renovating that one?" The place gives me the creeps. One wall is pretty much open to the elements, the floors and windowsills are rotten and the exterior paint hangs or curls in strips on the wood shingles. Photo albums remain, as do tattered curtains in the bedrooms, pots and utensils in the kitchen and a daybed in the front room. *Do not ask me about the bathroom upstairs ...*

"Waterfront," said Don. "Adjoining lot, also on waterfront. Secondary building beside the house, to be developed as the buyer sees fit. Last, the original home has the prettiest gingerbread on the island, I think. Lots of aesthetic and practical reasons to renovate this house."

"Mmmm," I said. "But you told me what people around here say about it – what was it again?"

He laughed: "'Gimme a can'a gas and a match, b'y, I'll look after it for yez.'"

"Still want to renovate it?"

"Yup. We start this autumn."

We. It was a word Don used a lot. Sometimes it was connected to me; mostly he connected the pronoun to Lulu and Mark, and to the people he knew on Isle Madame even before they came into his life. This time he was referring to his carpenter friend Edwin DeWolf and his assistant, my new friend, Murielle Vincent. This "we" may include me, too, this time, if I choose to be involved on the Mauger House renovation. I think I will.

Don's ties to this island are strong. He's lived here since 1971. He didn't meet Lulu, who lived abroad in Denmark for ten years, until the late '70s. But he knew Lulu's mother Mimi, has been close friends with her, since his earliest days here. They are another long-standing "we." So many years of we's before we married. For both of us.

Our "we's" are starting to blur, though. "Did I hear you say you liked curry?" Mimi had asked me several months ago. She is of Irish extraction, British, Brussels and Parisian raising, and a

Canadian war bride. She knows how to make a curry, one of my favourite foods.

"Yes," I answered. "I love them. My grandmother, my name-sake, used to make them for us."

"Right, then you and Don should come over for supper this week. I'll make a curry. Come on Wednesday, at 5:00. Don't be late."

She did, we did, and we weren't, and an unexpectedly lighthearted time was had by all. She greeted us with hugs.

Mimi has never once given me the "You're Not Lulu" stare I've had aimed at me so often since I met Don. Only some of these people are actually among Lulu's family, though for all of them, the stare is involuntary and usually only happens once. For me, it's like a just-pulled punch to my face, the air sucked back cold on all sides. When one of Lulu's siblings gave me the look the first time they met me, the silent room keened with the unfairness of death's crook. *Yes, I know,* I wanted to say, *I know damn well I shouldn't be here. She should.* Bravery? That sibling had boatloads of it. They couldn't speak much, couldn't smile at all, but stayed on for a short visit with Don and me anyway, for the fairness of it. *I know you know,* came the echo from those haunted eyes. *We're all doing our best.*

Back at Mimi's house that first night, the kitchen was warm with laughter and good will. Mimi was glad her "noble" son-in-law was loved again, I thought. As well, she seemed to like me, too. For me it was like being with my much-loved paternal grandmother, Marjorie Minnie again. Mimi's soft southern England vowels sounded so much like Minnie's voice. Mimi was just as girlish and charming, too.

"Chin-chin," toasted Mimi merrily, as we three clinked together our small glasses. The liquid was dark amber, set on ice.

"What is this lovely libation?" I giggled a short time later. I was already a bit tiddly, though my glass was still half-full. I had already asked what chin-chin meant – "It's a toast, of course," said Mimi, in her own circular, non-informative way – and no other explanation had followed. Perhaps I'd have better luck this time.

"A martini, of course," answered Mimi, dashing all my hopes for clarity. "What did you think?"

"But it's sweet," I said. "Can a martini be sweet?"

"Sweet or dry," said Don, "shaken or stirred, full or *empty*" – he set down his glass with a reluctant flourish – "they're all martinis."

Mimi was also giggling by now. "This is the Queen Mother's favourite drink," she told me. "Every evening at five, so they say."

Bloody good idea, was my thought. And it beats moonshine all to hell, was my next. I hadn't had nearly as much fun with that drink, on my first visit to D'Escousse. Too strong in effect and in flavour.

My first bite of the curry supper raised another question in my mind – but I was starting to feel silly, too inquisitive. Being unsure what meat was in the curry was just going to have to be another mystery. Didn't matter. It was delicious.

"Mmm," said Don. "Venison?"

"Yes," said Mimi. "One of the boys gave me some last autumn. Always makes a good curry."

I was thirty-nine years old and I'd never had curried venison. Marjorie Minnie, my grandmother, I am certain, would have enjoyed the one Mimi made that night. We – Don and I – certainly did. Minnie and Mimi even looked a bit alike, both tiny, bright-eyed, hair fine and wavy. Minnie had died in the late '70s. I hadn't met anyone remotely like her since then. Now I had. And this one made "Mimi Martinis," my instant name for the pre-supper drinks we would have again and again, whenever we – Mimi, Don and I – would share a meal together.

We. Don, Mimi and Marjorie. It's one of the nicest we's I have in my life.

## 25

### PASSAGES

#### MARCH 29, 2011, HALIFAX, NOVA SCOTIA

Still blowing and dark enough for lights on all over the house in the daytime. Dad was certain he suffered from SAD – Seasonal Affective Disorder – and certainly suffered from depression in the darker months of the year. I often wish his life had been easier, especially those last years. His wife Karin had set up house on her own by then and despite the fairness and love of their co-parenting, their two daughters were traumatized by the breakup of the marriage. Dad's health was also declining fast and hard. He kept on taking photos, though. He rarely lived a non-creative day.

Dad died on November 5, 1999. Guy Fawkes' Day, said his sister, our Aunt Susette, what a perfect day for him to leave us. Now every time we see the fireworks we'll think of him! *Bastard*, said his ex-wife, our mother Barbara, he left me again. Mum, I chastened, that's an awful thing to say. But she didn't retract or excuse the comment. A part of me approved of that. Mum was always a fighter.

My own anger had disappeared or been sublimated long ago. My last words to my father, whispered at his hospital bedside were, "I love you with all my heart." The world without Dad-letters, brimming with support and immense interest in his grown-up children's doings and writings, began.

Only another writer who loved us all – Dad included – could understand how desolate the loss of that letter-world felt to my sister Zoë, our brother Geoffrey and me. The man who had exchanged over eight hundred e-mails with me before our first kiss watched me walk to the post office across the street from our home in D'Escousse with a heart as heavy as mine. I'd come back to the house, hands empty, crying. Don, too, had received photo-cards from Dad. Don, too, knew how letters could throw stardust over the path of a sunless day. And perhaps only Don, too, could have kept up with the full blazing output of a Simmins correspondence, mine, in the first place. Of course I had to marry him.

Six months later, on September 23, 2000, Mum died. This death was unexpected – though not in retrospect, when all the signs of heart disease were discussed, became plain to see. We grown-up children knew something was off-kilter with Mum's health, had known for some time. Mum's doctor, however, an amiable oaf, stubbornly insisted all was well. In the end it was a stroke that took Mum from us. "The angels were with your mother," said the day nurse to a reeling and gutted Zoë, who had seen Mum alive and quite well only the evening before. "She went fast, wouldn't have known a thing."

The angels certainly smiled on me: the last thing I said to my mother, on the phone from Cape Breton to Richmond, was, "I love you." She died several days later. I had no clue I'd spoken to her for the last time. The world without mother-strength and love, vast, frigid and echoing, began. Don and I were in Vancouver in less than a day. I still don't know how we did that. This loss was different; it was in-the-bones elemental, could only be borne in reflection one blinkered moment at a time. Thought that edged out longer than that took feet to the edge of black-bottomed cliffs.

*We'll be all right, little love.*

How? How will we be all right? We need you. I want you and Don to spend more time together. I want you to know him better – be certain in your mother-mind that I am loved and cared for, and do this in return. That's the only reason I'd stick four thousand miles between us, Mum, you know that, right?

I don't understand – you were volunteering at a seniors' home just last week, had done for years. You weren't old, not in body nor outlook. Did you have to go?

*Loved being with you. See you.* We all agreed that Mum's epitaph was the most perfect we'd seen. Don particularly loved it. I particularly love him.

# 26

## The Event

### July 4, 2011, Halifax, Nova Scotia

I have considered these resuming words for ... over two months now. Two months and two days, nearly to the hour – and goddamned right I've been counting: I've never had my mobile life robbed from me before. In my thoughts I've started back to the writing with torrents of high drama and I've played with the briefest, most cryptic of descriptions. I've thought about words and images with a pounding, oversized heart. I've pushed myself far back from The Event on May 2 and I've shoved my face right back in the dirt I ate that day. I've told myself, "It's all grist for the [artist's] mill," as Dad told me time and again, when I was psychically or emotionally injured. The usually helpful dictate just made me feel worse and somehow that settled into the physical realm, primarily. But fear rarely left me, and despair nibbled around my body with bloodied rats' teeth.

First thought after the fall: *I am lying in a.pool of blood, from head to toe, cold, lapping blood, my own, it must be – what have I done?*

Fucking horse.

I moved my toes first, then my feet, hands, arms and head. Everything seemed to work. *Thank God, I am not paralyzed.* But I still couldn't move to sit up and I still didn't understand the sensation of liquid under my body. *Is something broken?* Pressed down by the full weight of the world-air above, I lay on my right side. My legs were slightly bent, my right arm was ... I am not sure, actually. I think it was under my head, the way you sometimes stick an arm under your pillow when you go to sleep. The water-blood feeling receded – then it was gone. I even felt comfortable, in a bizarre, frozen-in-time sort of way. As long as I didn't have to move or stand, I'd be fine. *Maybe I'll just lie here a while, chew on my dirt sandwich.*

Motherfucking horse.

I am calling out, and I am embarrassed, a useless lump of hurt woman who couldn't stay on her twenty-two-year-old schooling horse. *Help me! Help me! I need help!* I am surprised at how loud I am yelling. But I am alone in the big indoor arena and the only person who might hear me could be in the attached barn or could be well outside it, working in the other barn. What is her name again? Jen, her name's Jen. Nothing wrong with my head, apparently.

I hear her voice now. She's saying Hold on, I'll be right back. Got to get Buddy first – don't want him to trample you.

Trample me? Oh boy, hadn't thought of that. Is it a lie, then, that horses will do anything not to step on a person on the ground? That's what they told us when we were kids.

You are fifty-two years old now. You actually thought you could ride the way you did in your teens, twenties and thirties. Slim inside your middle-aged body, back supple and strong, hands and legs controlling twelve hundred pounds of unpredictable creature – no matter what happened.

*Fool.*

No, I won't accept that. I wasn't a fool. I damn near stayed on, too, at least at first. It was a dirty big bolt, a dirty big deke, and an endless high fall, like being shot out of a cannon from the top of a cliff. All because I decided to do one last canter around the ring and two seconds into that decision, a concussive blast of wind hit the plastic roof above us – and Buddy lost his mind. Adding to the excitement, he simultaneously remembered he was a Quarter horse, the breed that runs the fastest quarter-mile of any horse on the planet.

Even still, I truly believe I could have brought him back. I've brought back nightmare bolts on freight-train-heavy horses over the years. But that deke ... it wrenched my spine even before the ground wrenched and punched everything else. Very athletic manoeuvre for an old horse.

"Buddy?" squeaked the barn owner, Heidi. "Buddy dumped you?"

I didn't like Buddy's stable manners from the get-go, either – and the barn owner dismissed that, too. I think she'd seen him plod around the ring with beginner riders so many times – beginners who had nonetheless gotten his tack on without being bitten or kicked – and she just forgot he was capable of independent thought. Maybe Buddy is "sour," the term used for schooling horses that have worked too hard for too long. Sour horses can be angry horses. I think he was sore, too – maybe arthritis and certainly wear and tear on old bones and musculature. In the end he was just scared. He ran, turned hard – and left me behind. There was no intention to hurt.

Such a delicate emotional balance with horses: you love them at your delight and peril. As a horse friend of mine recently said, "As for horses, those pesky devils always manage to put those of us who would tame them in our place. They'll play along with us for the most part but in the end will take any opportunity to remind us and others that they are not dogs!"

No, they are not dogs – loyal, loving, biddable dogs. Though in truth all creatures can hurt us, given the right circumstances.

Buddy was only doing what horses have done since the dawn of their first day on earth: fear-based running, to ensure their survival.

You see how I am skirting around the hard stuff – talking mostly about horses, not me? I have just lived it, am still living it, can hardly bear to remember those shocking, new parameters of pain and dysfunction. What will I tell you about these past two months – that explains much, in brief?

I hate ambulances. I've only been in two – horses were the cause, both times. This time I was strapped on the full body board, with a big neck brace. My teeth chattered and I hyperventilated. They kept telling me to breathe slowly. One of the paramedics asked me if I'd like to hold his hand. *Oh yes please.* His hand was warm. I was frozen.

"You might find the morphine helpful," he suggested, some miles later, hand still in mine, as we slowly bumped down the country roads to the highway. Considering I was strapped down, I was able to squirm a fair bit. I couldn't help it, the neckbrace brought on major feelings of claustrophobia. I also thought, somehow, I could squirm right away from the agony.

"I don't do well with drugs," I said. "They scare me."

"Do you drink wine?"

"Yes."

"You know how you feel after you've had a glass – all relaxed?"

"Yes."

"Well, that's just the way the morphine will make you feel."

We went over a big bump. The world whited out into a pain blossom.

"All right. But I can't look at the needle."

I barely noticed the morphine's effects – but did find myself joking with the paramedics. I have no memory of the actual jokes. If I entertain these nice people, my addled brain decided, we can all pretend we're not in an ambulance – which is taking forever to get to the hospital.

At the hospital the doctors sent me off for x-rays. I cried out a lot as they moved me around. The world had never hurt me with every move before – or was that my own body, hurting me? No, impossible.

The nurses wheeled my gurney into a room, then lifted me onto a bed. Many drugs were proffered. A woman who can take morphine can take any painkillers – right? No, actually. Some drugs made me retch and try to vomit – oh, the pain! – some had no particular effect on pain or anything else. Finally, the attending doctor was happy with her selection for me: "Here's a prescription.

Take as directed." As for my malady: "You have no broken bones. You can go home now."

I couldn't walk, couldn't sit, couldn't rise to my feet or sink onto a toilet seat – but I was going home now. How on earth would I get off the bed? With help from Don, I slithered onto my knees, my arms braced against the side of the bed. Now what? Oh, God, the pain. I glared at the young doctor.

"You have soft-tissue injuries." For the first time, she looked sympathetic. "Soft-tissue and nerve injuries are complex – and take a long time to heal. Longer than broken bones."

My husband slipped his arms under mine, raised me to my feet. "Don't forget your prescription," said the doctor, handing Don the paper. "You'll need it."

Nerve pain: I didn't know such intense pain existed. Like swallowing an acid-coated lightning bolt. Day after day.

"Hold on tight, body like a noodle." These were Don's instructions to me each and every time he lifted me from the bed. I had to wrap my arms around his neck tight and close, so he wouldn't harm his back lifting me. But my body had to be a noodle, or the muscle spasming would start up, which it did, so often, for over a month. I was terrified of the spasming – which could fling me right off the toilet seat.

"Don, show me how a normal person gets off the toilet." All I could do was sit there, trying to remember which muscle did what when, and how your body actually rose from the sitting position. Once he had lifted me onto my feet and I was leaning against the doorway, Don showed me. I sighed. "Oh, you need your back to do it, not just your legs. That's why I can't do it. I have no strength in my back." A day later, Don installed a thick rope between the two stout handles on the wall across from the toilet. "I know you can't do it now, but soon, maybe." I practised reaching out my fingers to the rope, dreamed of pulling myself off the toilet again.

For two months, every single bit of normal in my life vanished: freelance writing, cooking, doing laundry and housework, grocery and retail shopping, wearing makeup and regular clothes, letter-writing and e-mail, reading, dog walks, showering, turning over in bed, pulling myself into a sitting position in bed, sleeping on my preferred side, the right side. When needed, I took narcotics, and was grateful for them. We ate every meal in our bedroom; I was propped up with pillows, used the bed tray, Don set a chair next to my side of the bed, ate with a plate on his lap. At supper time, Don would bring me a sherry glass of wine, set it on my bedside table. Later that evening he'd clear it away, still full, or down the three sips himself. "Are you sure you want me to keep pouring you a glass?" he'd ask. "Yes, it makes me feel like a normal person." Weeks passed. Water tasted best.

Don gave and gave and gave. *"For richer, for poorer, for better, for worse, in sickness and in health, as long as we both shall live …"* He lived the vows we'd recited thirteen years ago – and I thanked him, literally, every time he lifted me onto my feet. Other thank yous hummed in my bones: thank you for loving me; thank you for helping me; thank you for doing things nurses do and not being bothered; thank you for being great company; for making me good meals, for eating each of those with me – for keeping a glass of ice-water ever-present on the bedside table. *Thank you* for saying I am brave. Other than I love you, You are brave is my favourite thing to hear – of all things, ever.

I have tried to be so. And keep on trying.

On the darkest day of the injury I lay on my left side in bed, the newly purchased flat-screen television blatting at me from across the room. The skies themselves had been dark for weeks.

Put me in a soundproof closet, let me scream and pound my fists on the walls. I can't, I just *can't* lie here another day, the whys bouncing off my skull like blunt pebbles. *I didn't do anything wrong.* Why is so much of life the aftermath of *I didn't do anything wrong* – and I still can't bear the pain?

The words from the television soak into my mind like an ink stamp pressed on a snowy envelope: *You just never know what's around the next corner.* Goosebumps rise on my arms.

Mum? How many times did I hear you say that? You always said it with a wondering voice, as though we were all born to be delighted by wonderful surprises. Sometimes a subtext hummed in the air: *Don't worry, this too shall pass.* Sometimes, mostly, you said it to acknowledge the beautiful events that come to our lives. You had lots of those – and lots of other sorts, too.

Yet my mother's courage humbled me – even scared me once or twice, in its drone-like intensity.

*Don't go to that dark place*, she commanded me at another minute-by-minute time in my life. *You might not come back. Think about that. Wouldn't you rather be here in this world than gone, or your freedom taken from you? You can manage this, I know you can.*

*Two, four, six, eight* – yes, I can manage this.

## JULY 8, 2011, HALIFAX, NOVA SCOTIA

My Facebook posting for the day: "Last night I galloped my childhood Arabian horse over a wide grassy plain ... I lost my balance a little, he slowed – and all was gloriously well! We even took a jump or two, just for good measure!"

Holy God, that was a real dream. I even found myself counting the strides between the jumps; I was also aware, in a peripheral way, of how dry and yellowed the grass was. Very reminiscent of the summer day I rode my friend Jane's horse, Daisy, in Acme, Alberta. Daisy had been three-day eventing for several years with Jane at that point in the early '90s. Daisy was fit, keen and capable. Get on, said Jane, hopping off herself, take a jump or two. I didn't want to – why couldn't I just go for an easy hack? – but I never did know how to resist strong-willed Jane's "good ideas." Trust Daisy, she said, as I trotted away toward the first big fence, she knows what she's doing.

Three feet easy that jump was, with a big spread and another jump in a direct line from it, but a fair distance away. I knew without being told that honest Daisy would fly at the second one, so no chance of doing only one. What I didn't remember is that she would do both at a full gallop – that's what eventers do, gallop hard and fast over fences that do not move when hit – walls, really. Note to self: *don't hit.* Also: get off her face, give her enough rein to get over this monster and when in doubt, grab mane. *That's what God*

Back in the saddle: Marjorie riding Winnie the Quarter horse palomino, June 2013, Caberfeigh Stables, Dundee, Cape Breton, two years after the accident. (Photo by Silver Donald Cameron.)

*gave horses mane for,* screamed all my instructors over the years, *so hold onto it!*

Airspace: there was a lot of it between Daisy's tidy hooves and the stacked railway ties that formed the "jump." As predicted she landed on the other side and took off like a scalded cat to the second jump. I was so incidental to that mare's existence she might have been riderless.

Or was I? There's an honoured tradition of "packers" in the horse world: kind, big-hearted horses that "pack" their riders around with great care and in perfect safety – no matter what. Packers are generous to timid or inexperienced riders, or to those who might be rusty over fences, as I was that day.

*One, two, one, two* – airborne! *One, two, one, two, one, two* – we're in the sky!

Way to go! yelled Jane. Looked great! I didn't tell her my heart felt twisted with fear as much as swelled with satisfaction. I uncoiled my cramped fingers from Daisy's mane and came away with a tidy clump of strands. *Sorry, Dais ...*

There are few things nicer than a horse's loose, big-strided walk after a workout. The motion is self-congratulatory in the sunniest sort of way. It's also inclusive of the rider – who may or may not have much to congratulate herself on.

But I *stayed on*, didn't interfere with Daisy's work that day ... and yes, thoughts of *staying on* are cool hands on my sore back and battered right side. I am so lucky to have this memory-tape.

And all the other memory-tapes. Thank you, Daisy. Thank you, beloved Coqeyn. Thank you Boo, Kaber and Rory. Thank you all the horses of my life, with your bonfire hearts and nimble hooves – for carrying me so kindly, so safely across the years.

I will ride again – and not just in dreams and in memory.

27

## THE CITY GIRL IN THE CITY

*JULY 11, 2011, HALIFAX, NOVA SCOTIA*

The Canada Post strike this summer lasted over a month. Strange for me to be feeling cut off from the physical world in that time, and also cut off from my usual correspondents, primarily my friend Mimi and my brother Geoffrey. Without Don and MacTavish, it would have been a truly sunless world.

Now the letters are coming in again. One essential part of normal life (for a Simmins) has been re-instituted. The sun's back, too.

The letters that pass between my older sister Zoë, my younger sisters Jessica and Fiona and I tend to be irregular. They each write warm and informative letters and I feel lucky when I am the recipient.

Geoffrey and I write letters to one another frequently, infrequently and now and again; depends on the month and what's going on in our lives. We've been writing back and forth intensely and frankly for over thirty years, essentially dating from his move to Ontario after completing high school in Vancouver. He's been in Calgary since the late '80s.

Mimi and I have more traditional rules to our correspondence: once a week, stay upbeat, include family and general news. She and I have been writing one another since my earliest years in

D'Escousse, when Don and I were overwintering in B.C. for five years. After that, we kept on writing when Don and I sailed to the Bahamas, and finally, when we moved to Halifax in the autumn of 2006.

It's an unusual situation, I guess – but only to an outsider looking in. Mimi and I are fair-minded people; we can also, as luck would have it, live two impossible things before breakfast. In my case, I could love Don and be friends with Mimi – and be sad that Lulu had died and been taken from both of them. Mimi had known Don since he moved to D'Escousse in 1971; they'd been friends long before her daughter Lulu caught Don's eye in the early '80s. She just loved him more when he became her son-in-law. Unexpectedly but truly, Mimi liked me. I came to realize that when she called me her daughter's "successor," she was just being Mimi: truthful and a bit blunt. It was accurate, wasn't it? I was Lulu's successor. So I could be friends with my husband's late wife's mother – because we liked to eat curry, drink sweet martinis and chat easily about family and friends, near and far. The fact that we both loved Don simply deepened the friendship. Part of the reason I wrote Mimi letters was to make sure she always felt close to Don. More impossible reasoning: I thought it was a dirty trick of Fate she'd lost her daughter so young and unexpectedly; if Lulu couldn't keep Mimi up to date on Don's travels and life, then I would.

Nothing odd about that, is there?

My mother used to say that there are all sorts of things we worry about – that never ultimately transpire. Her point of course was to tamp down the worrying, as it serves no purpose at all. Mum occasionally took her own advice in this regard – and mostly could not. I am Barbara's daughter.

Don never did write the book about Lulu. I'd made it clear how uncomfortable I was with the idea and I know that unease counted. I like to think that Don had already done so much to honour Lulu's memory – organized an unprecedented, multi-denominational funeral and wake for her; built and planted a memorial garden; set up a scholarship fund in her name at Cape Breton University; written the words to a love song that was then set to music and recorded; archived her photos, letters, books and some of her personal possessions for her son, Mark, to name only a few things – that he didn't need to live in the sad place of writing a biography for his late wife. Maybe it wouldn't always have been a sad place, either, says the woman who retains her cavewoman ways. Either way, I am deeply grateful I didn't have to live with that. Don's intense, long-standing grief about Lulu did settle out over the years. I am glad for that, too. I'd have to be a stupid and ungrateful woman not to know how well I am loved and cherished ... by Lulu's husband, Mark's dad and Mimi's son-in-law.

Nothing odd about that, either. I came to our marriage with a past, too. How could we not have had past lives? We were thirty-nine and sixty-one years old when we married.

"I think you and Lulu could have been good friends," Don was fond of saying for many years. I'd nod and smile and think, perhaps, perhaps not. We always want the people we love to love each other, too – and it doesn't happen as often as we'd like. It's hard for me to remember how it felt to look at Don as someone else's husband. Meeting his high-spirited Acadian wife when I was simply West Coast Marjorie might have been great, uncomplicated fun. I will never know.

About other, actual events I have firm opinions. That long-ago summer evening on Don's sailboat *Silversark* – I am certain Lulu kissed my cheek in gratitude. These non-dreaming incidents have happened to me all my life; I've never denied their validity and never will. Mum spoke to me just the other week, when the darkness crowded in on me. As for the basement nightmare, that was my own psyche pulling out the big guns, to help me start to think about leaving Cape Breton. I loved the region and its peoples in many ways: the Celtic music and culture, the Mi'kmaq communities and events, the powerful geography on such a small island, the quilting, country auctions, sailing in the Bras d'Or Lakes and throughout Isle Madame's surrounding archipelago, and the stunning autumn palette in the Highlands. My cherished friends: Denise Saulnier; Ann Delorey, who is the lilting voice and big, smiling heart of Cape Breton at its finest (and her whole charming family); and

Murielle Vincent, whose life-grace and non-judging heart humble me like no other person I know. With Murielle I have laughed so hard I've had to beg for the mercy of one indrawn breath: *Stop it, stop it, you're killin' me!* And still she has "tormented" me, as a Caper would gleefully use the word, and made me laugh more.

But I was not to the country born, and never felt comfortable with the community power struggles and dominant cliques. Mostly I missed the privacy or anonymity available in a city, and disliked how days or evenings could be stolen from you by those who came to the house and expected social time: *now*, please. I cooked hundreds of meals for hundreds of people; gave small parties, medium parties, parties so big I felt oddly like a teenager again. I chose to do this, was not pressured by Don to do so. I thought it was what a new wife and a new community member should do. I didn't know how to draw back when I got tired and resentful. Oddly, we weren't asked out that often to other people's homes. This may have been due to our intense friendship with Greg and Denise. Perhaps other people thought our social needs were covered in that one close relationship. Regardless, we mostly saw island people at community events.

Then I stopped writing. It didn't happen overnight and I did some good, publishable work in the early Cape Breton years. My interest was piqued by the house renovations Don did; I joined his crew on these projects. Our own house renovations took a long time to finish; we did this as money and time became available. I could only just keep up to the front, back and side gardens at our house, but I did, most years. Don did everything he could to find me a horse to ride; it just didn't work out. I made no money and felt useless and dependent. For someone who had made money since she was sixteen, had always had enough to get by and to occasionally help out family members or friends, it was humiliating to never have a payday. I felt lower than dirt.

Then my thyroid died – I became "hypothyroid." I didn't know anything about the thyroid and its functions. All I knew was that I could barely crawl up the stairs after lunch for a lie-down. The "nap" would last two or three hours. I awoke exhausted. My ankles ached, my skin dried all over my body and my menstrual periods were, for the first time in my life, painful and heavy. Depression settled heavy as canvas on my back. I was bewildered and scared by the depression – and worried: is this what middle age felt like, bleak and hopeless? Medication soon alleviated the worst of these symptoms.

And still I did not write. In eight years I'd gone from specialist (fisheries) to generalist (personal essays and articles) to silent. I'd stopped riding, and lost my father and mother a scant six months apart. I worked on acceptance of my childless life with a volcanic heart and despite new friends, I missed my other "kids" – my childhood and university girlfriends in Vancouver. The woman in the mirror who stared back at me each morning was a stranger. I was getting close to detesting every aspect about her. The only recognizable and lovable feature to her was her dog, Leo.

*"I love the whippet and the whippet loves me, oh yes he does,"* I'd sing as I walked along the rocky beach below our house. Leo would trot ahead of me, just a short ways, checking over his shoulder every few minutes to see I was keeping up. Usually, as Zoë had written about in her wedding poem for Don and me, he carried a stick, one much too large for him. I'd smile at that beloved deer-face and in those moments of soft affection I'd permit entry to my heart of all the beauty around me: late-in-the day lilac and gold skies; the spikes of evergreens on a nearby island; the grey shadows of blue herons; the sudden white among dark stones of a broken marble headstone, which had toppled from the graveyard above the beach. Sometimes I could make out a surname, or if incomplete, guess at it.

*LeBlanc, Boudreau, Poirier, Terrio, Samson, Dewolf, Marchand, DeCoste, Petitpas, Richard* – I could cite most of the region's original Acadian names now – and some of the Jersey Island, Basque and Irish ones, particular to Isle Madame: Janvrin, LeVesconte, Bourinot, LeBrun, Mauger, Goyetche, Baccardax, Kehoe, Doyle and O'Hearn. I had loved learning so much about Isle Madame, Cape Breton, the Maritimes and Atlantic Canada – I'd been a hungry student of life for near-on a decade – but suddenly I felt as though I were disappearing, becoming blurry around the edges. Every identifying tag in my life had changed. My mind bulged with the lives and histories of others – but I, as Silver Don's wife and a Come-From-Away westerner, was mostly one-dimensional. I had a family, but they were too far away to be of any interest to others. So while I could chat easily about the lives of literally hundreds of islanders, Mimi's nine children and all of their children included, no one asked me about my family. Ever. It made me miss them even more.

*Me, me, me,* what about me? Why this, why that, why can't I turn off the discontented chatter-mill in my mind, even for a single day? If something didn't happen soon, I was headed for a screaming departure from the East Coast and possibly my marriage.

Something did happen. Don's heart attack. July 4, 2006. About 6:30 p.m.

Five years after the fact, we don't call it a heart attack anymore. After all the terror and relief (me), after all the research, testing, doctors' appointments, procedures and calmness (Don), after all the megawatt confusion of moving to Halifax from Cape Breton mere weeks after Don ended up in the ICU of St. Martha's in Antigonish (both), Don's heart specialist pronounced that Don had had a "heart episode." Yes, he had blockage in the right main artery; but no, not bad enough for surgery. No, blood tests did not indicate a true heart attack; yes, he'd now be on medications to prevent future "episodes" or, God forbid, a serious heart attack.

Oh, you came to the city because of access to better medical care, said person after person who blinked with surprise to see Silver Donald Cameron in the city – on the "Mainland," if you please. Everyone knew his heart was in Cape Breton – *Isle Madame, particulièrement* – for ever and always. No, said Don forcefully, our medical care in Cape Breton is excellent. Between Antigonish and Sydney, and the occasional appointment in the city, we could have managed the situation. We came to Halifax because it was the right move for Marjorie.

*Me, me, me* ... It still seems like I was being so selfish, and yet what would I have done in Cape Breton if a heart attack had claimed Don's life? The Telile apartment building, the Morrison House, our big marital home – what would I have done about all these properties? Yes, I had friends. But no family anywhere close by, and the nearest large airport was three and a half hours away. I wasn't working, wasn't writing, wasn't happy, wasn't growing intellectually or emotionally and was feeling more claustrophobic and held back by the second. We still lived with Lulu's archive, for God's sake, and Mark's childhood possessions and library.

It was Don who suggested we move to the city; I had tried the suggestion in years past, and had been glared down. Intellectually, I understood that Don had a complicated business presence on the island. The apartment and house-rental businesses had taken him years to build and would take years to disassemble, when the decision to do so was made. The businesses also supported us, far more than our writing at the time did. I also understood how deep his ties were to the island and its residents. He is never happier than when he is home on Isle Madame. Emotionally, however, I was climbing the walls for change. Regardless, I certainly wasn't going to start a campaign for moving or anything else, after the summer we'd been through. So after all the fear of losing him, all the physical closeness and emotional connection of the post-episode days, I could barely take in what Don was saying to me: 24 Armshore Drive; it's on the water; I could live here and be happy; with income from the downstairs suite, we can just afford it. *Do you like it?*

Do I like it? Dear God, I would have been thrilled with an ancient bungalow on a busy street, or an apartment somewhere near the city. Do I like this three-bedroom Georgian-style home facing the Northwest Arm at the western edge of the city I loved on sight, that first trip to the Maritimes in 1996?

Yes. Every day, in every way. Professionally and personally, I've hardly set a foot wrong since we came to live here. In June 2008, I completed a Certificate Course in Adult Education at Dalhousie University. The course was wonderfully stimulating and brushed up my rusty teaching skills. In 2009, I started teaching memoir writing to seniors (and others) again. I am freelancing regularly for publications I want to be published in, about subjects I want to write about. At the end of this year I will have finished a Master of Arts Research, specializing in Memoir Studies, from Mount Saint Vincent University. My ten-year dream of getting an MA is coming true – and is far better and more exciting an experience than I had hoped or imagined. Also important to me is that I once again feel *au courant* with urban trends and popular culture, a strength I am able to incorporate into my writing, as my dad had once noted.

The move to the city was no Pyrrhic victory, either. It looks like our big blue house in D'Escousse will sell this summer, but with our Cape Breton foothold, the small Victorian-era Morrison House, still in our holdings, Don is content with our city home. Far best of all, Don's health is excellent. Our diet has improved, he is fit from exercise and walks and all sorts of good work has come his way, too.

## 28

## STILL HEALING

### JULY 17, 2011, HALIFAX, NOVA SCOTIA

My right foot is still numb and has nasty pins and needles around the edges. It makes it hard to walk or feel steady on my feet. As for getting around, I lurch more than anything, which is hard on my back. At least I don't have to use the cane any more. Patience is what I am working hardest on now. I want my regular life back – want every enjoyable speck of it back, from dog walks to hikes to long mornings in the kitchen, chopping and stirring and smacking shut the oven, fridge and cupboard doors. I do most of these things in tiny measure now – I just want more. And yet the last of the nerve injury, currently residing in the foot, will not be rushed. What was it my dear grade three teacher Mrs. Harris used to say? "When in a hurry, take plenty of time." It's a useful platitude.

On a cheerier note, Don and I did something normal and fun just yesterday: we went to a movie matinee downtown. We saw Woody Allen's forty-first (!) movie, *Midnight in Paris*. It was charming! We loved everything about it: the cinematography (a love song to The City of Love), the cast (anyone who's anyone, *dahling*, would sum it up), the amusing, crisp dialogue and the delicious time travel. We were also intrigued by the movie's central premise, that few people are really happy with the era in which they grew up, or perhaps even their spot in time throughout their lives. Allen has two of his main characters dazzle-eyed for the '20s (our hero) and the turn-of-the-nineteenth-century "Golden Age" (our heroine), though both live disaffectedly in other times. Both are certain their lives would be shimmering, pure magic, had they only been born in the "right" decade. Allen's final word on that yearning: rubbish. You have the life you have. If it isn't the way you want it to be, then change it. Our hero ultimately does just this – changes his life – and lo and behold, a new, suitable and attainable woman appears beside him. His decisiveness is instantly rewarded.

And it all rang true, for these two moviegoers.

"Do not get me started on how much I detested the '50s," Don has said to me time and again. "Conservative, racist, crappy music, sexually stifling. In a word, stultifying. The '70s were a gale of fresh air."

"Ha! The '70s were a locomotive off the tracks," I always reply. "Feminist and colour-blind in word only, warping and weird pop psychologies, crappier music, sexually hyperactive and demented. Way too many drugs, too much drinking. In a word, overwhelming. The stolid, safe '50s would have suited me fine."

We grin at each other, quite unwilling to give our separate decades the smallest bit of slack.

And yet and of course ... these decades shaped us. As we grew older, we appraised our eras' teachings and sorted out what we wanted, and discarded the rest. There are even features of the '70s I now look back on with affection. We were active teenagers – walking, hiking, riding horses and our fancy "10-speeds" all over the city of Vancouver. After years spent competing in and then watching horse shows, we young women also loved to "wahoo" at the top of our lungs – any excuse to voice life joy and vigour. Our code phrase for any adventure we took on was, "Let's get into it!" We wrote, sketched, painted, loved live theatre and our local dingy pool hall. We had no "off" buttons.

Overall, I believe that our times in history, anyone's time in history, is only as special as the people who come and go in it, and the places you are able to call home. In this regard, Don and I are blessed. We have one another, and two sets of families and friends who bring us joy. We love, as our friend Sandra Delorey said, wherever we go on the East and West Coasts, and spots in between. And are loved.

That's a lot of love.

*29*

## PARTING WITH HELLOS

"Part with hellos" – I used this phrase in the essay I wrote about Dad, which was published in *Canadian Living* in 1996. For the first time in a lifetime of visits, I wasn't frightened to walk away from my father, knew I'd see him again, knew there would be more shared laughter and stories. If I'd known there were only three years left in his lifetime, I would have been frightened again. Instead, I walked away from him marvelling at my lack of tears, the lightness of my heart. A sweet, unforgettable moment.

I need to part with another hello – here, now, amidst these one-after-another words. There's so much more I'd love to write about here – but of course I do, that's how a writer makes sense of the world, day by day, year by year. *Marjorie,* says my thesis advisor gently, *this is a memoir you are writing, not an autobiography.* She is right.

So why is my heart racing?

Because I need to know – this time, have I Made It Right? Have I made the story right? There were so many times, as a child, as an adult, that I could not will into being certain outcomes. There was magic all around me – in the rainbows, in the fistfuls of mane atop galloping horses, in the sailing adventures of Three Forever, in the current voices of love and the remembered voices of our ancestors, in the unexpected, middle-world touch and words of others – and yet I could not always ease the pain of those around me, or accept with grace the biggest plot twists in my own life.

You couldn't live a perfect life or perfect the lives of others – is that what you're saying? Who can? Who would want to?

That would be Don – saucy fellow, I didn't know he could hear me writing today. He's upstairs at his desk, I'm downstairs at mine. It's mid-morning and I've already e-mailed him a couple of times.

*Is today the day? Have you finished the memoir?*

I think so. But I am a little worried.

*You, worried. What have you done with my real wife?*

I am your real wife, the one and only Miss Cheerywinky. Seriously, I am worried that I've missed something – maybe even something important.

*You have.*

What do you mean?

*It's the nature of a life story, or a life chapter, as a memoir is. We will always leave out something important – probably several or many importants. It doesn't matter. You're not supposed to record every sniffle or snivel. You're supposed to tell stories, carve out your own small presence in the world and share your thoughts about that world. Have you done that? Do you agree?*

Yes, and yes. But Don, this is an imaginary conversation.

*Does it seem that way to you?*

No. But it is.

*Fine, you want real, phone me. I believe it's your turn.*

Sniffle or snivel, he says – honestly, just *wait* till I – where is that phone, anyway?

"Hello?" he says – his voice as warm as ever.

"Hello," I say – "it's me."

# Epilogue

## June 2013, Halifax, Nova Scotia

We walked in Point Pleasant Park yesterday – me, the Silver Scribe and the eight-footed Orange Brigade. That's right, we have two amber-hued or "sable" Shetland sheepdogs now. Franki, the new female Sheltie, is officially registered as "Talisker's Frankly Speaking." She is as effervescent as a pétillante wine and as playful as an otter. With her arrival in March of this year, we humans and our beloved Tavie – officially, "Talisker's Seadog MacTavish" – (from the same breeder) indisputably became a pack.

Just as my West Coast dog friends always told me, being a pack is a particular and intense joy.

It is also a joy to forget, for hours at a time, that I ever had a horseback riding accident so severe that I might not have walked again, or might have dealt with chronic pain or disability for the rest of my life.

Yesterday, deep in the sun-latticed woods that are still recovering from Hurricane Juan in 2003, I felt exactly the way I felt on the morning of May 2, 2011, as I dressed to spend a day at the barn: limber and heedless – untouchable by malevolent gods. This is our human birthright, I believe, to stride into each day, believing the world will welcome, not wound, us. Unlike that chilly, portentous spring day, yesterday was fragrant summer perfection. In that place of forest healing, warm air circled around us, pushed by seasonally mild breezes off the Atlantic. I could breathe deeply with no pain or discomfort; I literally grew taller, breathing into the lost half-inch of height taken from me two years and one month ago, retrieved by walking and stretching. Around us Haligonians walked dogs of every type, breed and age. Don held MacTavish's leash, I held Franki's leash. We walked along, hips grazing, two Maritimers and their dogs.

Becoming a pack: Marjorie, MacTavish, Don and Frankie, Halifax, Nova Scotia, November 2013. (Photo by Chris Beckett.)

## About The Author

Marjorie Simmins is an award-winning writer based in Halifax, Nova Scotia. Raised in Vancouver, she has worked as a freelance journalist, editor and writing instructor for over twenty years, writing often about family, marine life, animals and coastal living. Her articles and essays have appeared in magazines and newspapers across Canada and the U.S. and in several anthologies.

In 1994, she won a Gold Medal at the National Magazine Awards for a memoir-article published in *Saturday Night*. In 2012, she won Gold at the Atlantic Journalism Awards for the Best Atlantic Magazine article. Her most current anthology contribution was a memoir-essay that appeared in *Untying the Apron: Daughters Remember Mothers of the 1950s*, published by Guernica in 2013.

Simmins currently writes primarily for periodicals and teaches memoir writing courses around the Maritime region. She has a Master of Arts Research, specializing in Memoir Studies, from Mount Saint Vincent University in Halifax, and offers memoir manuscript evaluations via her website, Memoirs and More, www.marjoriesimmins.ca. Simmins lives with "her pack," husband Silver Donald Cameron and their Shetland sheepdogs, MacTavish and Franki.